Jan Oliver Schwarz, Felix von Held
Robust Leadership

Jan Oliver Schwarz, Felix von Held

Robust Leadership

Leading with Confidence into an Uncertain Future

DE GRUYTER

ISBN 978-3-11-224279-7
ISBN 978-3-11-224280-3 (PDF)
ISBN 978-3-11-224281-0 (EPUB)
DOI https://doi.org/10.1515/9783112242803

Library of Congress Control Number: 2026936499

Bibliographic information published by the Deutsche Nationalbibliothek
The Deutsche Nationalbibliothek lists this publication in the Deutsche Nationalbibliografie; detailed bibliographic data are available on the Internet at http://dnb.dnb.de.

De Gruyter and Walter de Gruyter GmbH are part of De Gruyter Brill.
www.degruyterbrill.com

Questions about General Product Safety Regulation:
productsafety@degruyterbrill.com

Cover illustration: Günther G. Hoffmann

Acknowledgments

This book is the result of many conversations, reflections, and shared insights. We are deeply grateful to everyone who contributed their ideas, challenged our thinking, and supported the development of both the study and this manuscript. Robust leadership was shaped not in isolation, but through dialogue and collaboration.

Before publishing this English edition, we had the privilege of releasing a German version of the book. Since then, we have applied the robust leadership framework in numerous workshops, leadership programs, and keynote presentations. The thoughtful feedback, critical questions, and encouraging responses we received from practitioners and leaders across industries have significantly strengthened and refined our approach. Their experiences and insights have helped us further sharpen the framework presented in this book.

First and foremost, we extend our heartfelt thanks to our families. Their patience, encouragement, and unwavering support gave us the time, space, and freedom required to bring this project to life. Without them, this book would not exist.

The visualizations, which are central to the robust leadership framework, would not have been possible without the exceptional work of the IICM design team. We are especially grateful to Lisa von Pflugk, Anastasiia Korzh, and Ellina Kollmer for translating complex ideas into clear and compelling visual forms.

We would also like to express our special appreciation to Annabel Zettl, whose expertise and professional background significantly enriched the development of our models and sharpened the overall concept of the book. Prof. Dr Bernhard Wach played a pivotal role in the evaluation of our two studies, providing academic rigor and thoughtful guidance. Our sincere thanks also go to Dr Felix Werle. The intensive discussions and practical applications we developed together – particularly in connection with the first robust leadership study – laid an essential foundation for this work.

To all who accompanied us on this journey: thank you for your trust, your insights, and your commitment.

 | https://doi.org/10.1515/9783112242803-202

Contents

Abbreviations

AI	Artificial intelligence
IICM	Institute for Innovation and Change Methodologies
IT	Information technology
OKR	Objectives and key results
TUNA	Turbulence, uncertainty, novelty, ambiguity
VUCA	Volatility, uncertainty, complexity, ambiguity

 | https://doi.org/10.1515/9783112242803-204

1 Introduction

Questions addressed in this chapter:

- What is the background of the robust leadership framework?
- How does the framework help me as a leader?
- What are the challenges for leadership in the future?

What is effective leadership? And how can effective leadership contribute to the performance of an organization or team? For us, these two questions are central in discussions of leadership. While leadership as an issue for research, teaching, or development has been around for decades, and people have been recognized as leaders since the first societies, what leadership needs to be is discussed and redefined constantly, especially given the changing contexts in which organizations find themselves.

Over half a century ago, management guru Peter Drucker (1969) argued that the "age of discontinuity" had begun, and that change was occurring more rapidly than in the past. Organizations face a more complex and dynamic environment than ever, one that is characterized by discontinuities and an uncertain future – a state that is most likely to continue. The major tasks for leaders today are to make decisions, formulate strategies, and execute strategic management systems in changing environments. It is obvious that the imperative of "predict and prepare," the foundation of the neoclassical school of management (Gharajedaghi 1999), is no longer appropriate.

The financial crisis of 2008, the COVID 19 pandemic, developments in the area of Artifical Intelligence (AI) and of course the war in Ukraine demonstrate that organizations are faced with a VUCA environment. In recent years, the acronym VUCA (volatility, uncertainty, complexity, and ambiguity) has been used to frame the challenges the organizations face. Rafael Ramirez and Angel Wilkinson (2016) from the Said School of Business at Oxford University have coined the acronym TUNA (turbulence, uncertainty, novelty, and ambiguity), suggesting that we have already moved beyond VUCA in terms of increasingly uncertain and dynamic business environments.

In this context, it has been argued that the leadership skills needed to lead an organization with a stable, supportive environment are not identical to the skills needed to lead an organization in a VUCA environment (Yukl and Gardner 2020). A more recent study, informed by the COVID-19 pandemic, finds that board members on the one hand see their role in providing long-term orientation for their organization, but on the other hand many board members do not believe that

 | https://doi.org/10.1515/9783112242803-001

they are adequately contributing to the future preparedness of their organizations (Gordon, Jonasson, and Larsen 2021). Some organizations perceive these dynamics as a risk, others as an opportunity – and still others as both. One question, however, is critical for all organizations: What kind of leadership culture can help them to rise to this challenge?

In his seminal book *The Reflective Practitioner*, first published in the early 1980s, Donald A. Schon (2008) argues that managers have become increasingly sensitive to the phenomena of uncertainty, change, and uniqueness. He contends that since the 1960s, "decision-making under uncertainty" has become a common term in leadership. However, how have these insights been reflected in leadership theory and practice?

John P. Kotter (2012) of the Harvard Business School and a thought leader in the field of change management has argued that leading change is one of the most important and daunting responsibilities for managers and administrators. Leading change entails guiding, encouraging, and facilitating the collective efforts of members to adapt and survive in a VUCA environment. And while we assume that the state of VUCA will increase and that any effort, be it developing a new strategy or being more innovative, will inevitably include change, the relevance of leadership in this context also increases. In other words, while the business environment is growing increasingly challenging for organizations and their leaders, the responsibility to provide orientation for leaders also increases. This implies that if leadership fails to provide orientation despite an increasing need to change, organizations risk falling out of alignment with their business environment. And of course, many stakeholders are desperately seeking answers. Whether battling bureaucracy in organizations (Hamel and Zanini 2020) or organizing for the "new normal" (Markides 2021), this list could be endless.

We are especially eager to explain what it means to provide orientation as leaders in such an environment. We will offer our own perspective on leadership, which we term *robust leadership* (Figure 1).

For us, robustness goes beyond resilience. For us, *robustness* not only means being able to deal with the changes in the organizational environment but actually to use these changes as opportunities. And while some might perceive a VUCA environment primarily as risky and challenging to adapt to, others might see these dynamics as an opportunity to develop new business models, to design new business or services, or to reposition their organization. Two decades ago, Paul Schoemaker's and Robert Gunther's (2002) book *Profiting from Uncertainty: Strategies for Succeeding No Matter What the Future Brings* observed that uncertainty is a source for profits. Nassim Nicholas Taleb (2012) pointed in a similar direction with his concept of antifragility. Further, for us robustness means striking the right balance in adapting to changes in the business environment and proving stability, providing orientation

Figure 1: Robust leadership and the VUCA environment.

for the members of an organization. Regardless of the direction in which a leader is taking his or her organization, navigating the VUCA world is a challenge which is most likely not going to go away. New technology trends will emerge, customer preferences will continue to change, and new trends will appear.

Robust leadership provides a central stabilizing mechanism for organizational value creation, whether in terms of performance or of organizational de-

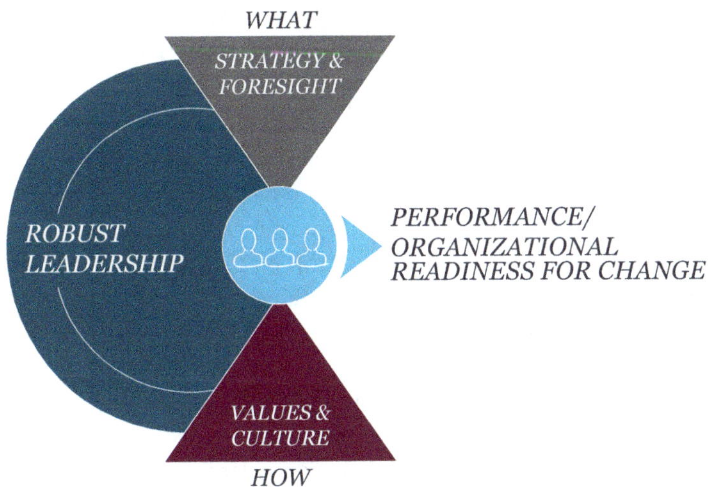

Figure 2: Robust leadership framework.

velopment. Robust leadership (Figure 2) is characterized by providing orientation in terms of *what* an organization shall achieve (strategy and foresight), and *how* this shall be achieved (values and organizational culture).

1.1 Motivation for This Book

In an interview with Forbes, leadership expert Professor Jeffrey Pfeffer from Stanford was asked why the leadership industry has failed in making workplaces better and leaders more effective. He responded: "I see at least two huge problems. First, anyone can be leadership expert with no knowledge of the relevant social science, no expertise, no experience required" (Schawbel 2015). The second huge problem was the insufficient approaches to measuring the effectiveness of leadership trainings.

In his groundbreaking book *Leadership BS*, Pfeffer (2015: 3–4) takes issue with the leadership industry:

> Over time, a largely unchanging, sometimes research-based set of recommendations for how to improve group and organizational performance emerged. The recommendations include, but are not limited to, that leaders inspire, trust, be authentic, tell the truth, serve others (particularly those who work for and with them), be modest and self-effecting, exhibit empathic understanding and emotional intelligence, and other seemingly sensible nostrums. And on the other hand, there sits ample, even overwhelming evidence of workspaces filled with disengaged, dissatisfied employees who do not trust their leaders and whose oft-expressed number one desire is to leave their current employer.

While one can argue that in recent years the number of concepts, such as innovation leadership, agile leadership, or design leadership, has only increased, in this book we present a framework that rests on the two pillars of research and practice.

Our motivation for this book stems from two sources. In past years, we have investigated leadership by conducting two studies on robust leadership along with our research in this field. Our first study, carried out in early to mid-2020, was more exploratory. We wanted to understand how our robust leadership framework resonates with leaders and how the elements of our framework are interconnected form an empirical perspective. Our second study, done in 2022, was more quantitative and explored the interrelationships of the elements of our robust leadership framework. We collected insights from approximately 500 business leaders.

In our work with many leaders in our consulting practice, we have started to think about how we can structure our thoughts around leadership. Developing the robust leadership framework helped us to engage more meaningfully with our clients in supporting them to thrive in a VUCA environment.

The robust leadership framework is, of course, a framework. This means that we are not answering all questions about leadership. This book is not a leadership bible. We are providing a framework which we perceive more as a reference point. We sincerely hope that this framework supports you and your organization in structuring your thoughts around leadership. We have consciously chosen approaches to be used in this framework, but you are free to add your own ideas and thoughts on how to apply robust leadership.

For whom is this book intended? Basically, anyone who leads a small or large organization in the private or public sector. Our aim is to provide a practical guide for leadership. That means that this book contains many exercises and reflections which can be done individually or in a group. However, we want to ensure that this book has a solid foundation, and we cite the academic literature or rely on our empirical research.

We embark on our journey (see Figure 3 for the structure of the book) by explaining in this chapter not only why our robust leadership framework is relevant but also by introducing it and describing some of its mechanisms. In the chapter on leadership tensions, we reflect on results from our first study on robust leadership. We identify key types of tension that leaders need to address to ensure organizational success and longevity, particularly in times of change. With tensions we refer to challenges and issues which arise due to conflicting ways of dealing with certain situations – triggered by VUCA – from a leadership perspective. We follow this discussion by describing the robust leadership framework in more detail and highlighting how one can become a robust leader.

We then describe how the concept of robust leadership can be applied to organizations, making them robust. This means that we are considering two perspectives in our discussion on robust leadership: individual and organizational. And while of course these two perspectives are interrelated, we will address them both with our robust leadership framework. With our robust leadership assessment, readers can evaluate the robustness of their individual and organizational leadership styles. In the last chapter we wrap up by tying leadership tensions to our robust leadership framework.

We recommend that you read this book chapter by chapter, following our structure and journey. Do not just consume the content of this book; engage with our concept of robust leadership. We have included several reflection exercises and our robust leadership assessment tool. These supplemental materials will give you some ideas on how you can use this book not only to reflect on your own leadership practice but also to work with your colleagues or teams on developing robust leadership.

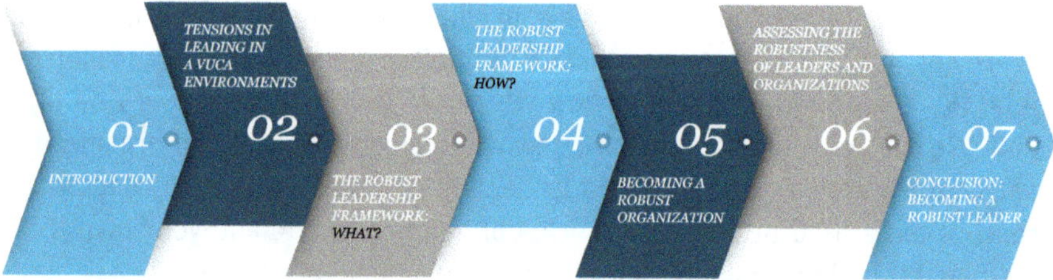

Figure 3: Structure of the book.

1.2 The Future of Leadership

Our robust leadership framework is suited to address the many challenges posed by the VUCA world. However, if we consider that pressures on leadership will only increase, it becomes even more evident that new mechanism are needed. To better understand what possible challenges for leadership in a VUCA world could be, we will discuss scenarios on the future of leadership.

The scenarios we are describing here were developed by one of the authors in collaboration with master's students at the ESB Business School in Reutlingen, Germany. The task at hand was to explore the context of leadership in the future, meaning how organizations could look like 2030. The project followed the approach to developing scenarios, originally developed at Royal/Dutch Shell 50 years ago (van der Heijden 1996). The underlying rationale of the scenario planning approach is that the future, in particular the longer-term future, cannot be predicted. Describing the future therefore can only mean developing alternative and plausible pictures of the future, describing the range of possibilities, and not trying to predict a single outcome.

We will not describe the development of the scenarios in detail. Instead, we will use the description of the scenarios to emphasize our point that the challenges facing leadership will most likely increase.

Figure 4 shows an overview of selected trends used in the development of the scenarios on the future of leadership. The starting point for the creation of scenarios is the identification of those drivers which are both relevant for the future of leadership and uncertain. Uncertainty in this case refers to the assessment that it is unclear in which direction a trend might develop and that these directions might also be opposite.

In this project, the following two uncertainties were identified: (1) blurring lines between private and work life; and (2) artificial intelligence.

Figure 4: Selection of drivers for the future of leadership.

The blurring lines between private and work life were as follows:
- The COVID-19 crisis shows that employers are a safety net for many employees, in terms of financial, mental, and physical well-being.
- Companies are part of the employees' social environment by, for instance, facilitating social interaction at after-work events, providing insurances and childcare.
- These activities support employer branding activities and seem to enable a better work-lifebalance.

Artificial intelligence is identified as follows:
- Technology driven by artificial intelligence will be placed in different use cases in business environment to digitize processes.
- Robots will work autonomously; however, failure times will be caused by technical issues only humans can repair.

- Employees will have to collaborate more with robots than with their human coworkers.

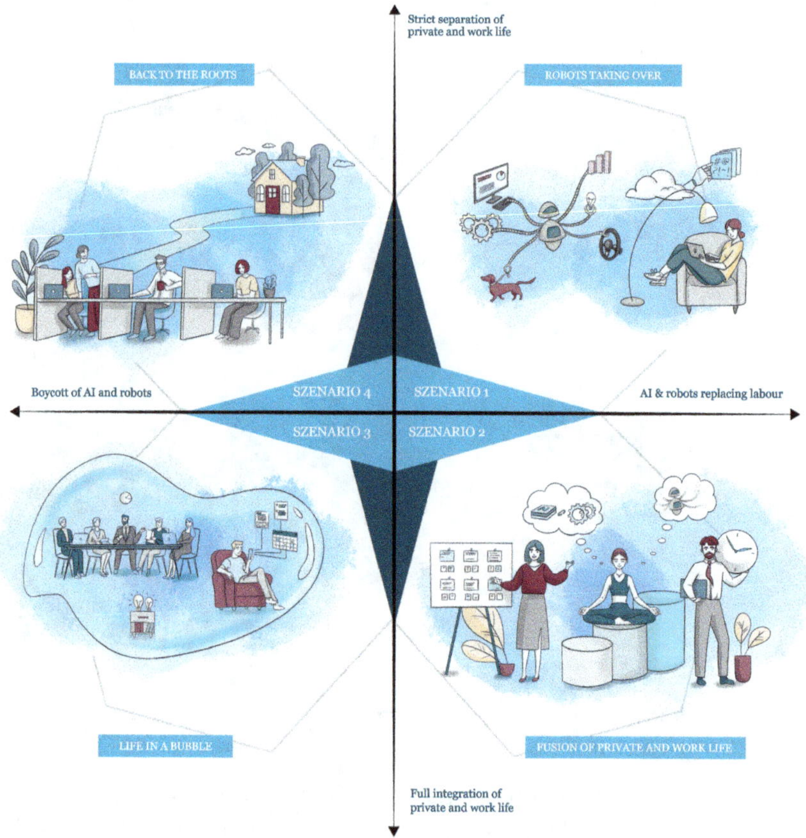

Figure 5: Scenarios on the future of leadership.

Figure 5 displays the developed scenarios in which besides the key drivers, all other trends were combined to plausible and alternative pictures of the future. In the following, we briefly describe these four worlds.

1.2.1 Scenario 1: Robot Takeover

What does a world look like in which robots and AI replace a large part of the workforce and work and private life are strictly separated (Figure 6)?

- Everyday life has changed significantly in recent years. Technological advances are enabling robots and AI to take over 80% of the work previously done by humans.
- There are clear boundaries between work and private life. In the event of errors, these lead to long downtimes for the robots and AI.
- Executives are confronted with controlling and monitoring automatisms, end users of instructions are no longer people, but robots or AI.

Figure 6: Scenario 1: "Robot Takeover".

1.2.2 Scenario 2: Fusion of Private and Work Life

What does a world look like in which robots and AI have replaced a large part of the workforce and where work and private life are integrated (Figure 7)?

- The world is changing. Robots and AI are replacing almost all manual human workstreams.
- The human workforce is geared toward navigating, monitoring, and programming robots and AI.
- Workers can organize their work and free time flexibly but must be available 24/7 to be able to intervene with robots or AI in an emergency.
- Executives are confronted with the blurring of private and work life. The main task is to maintain the motivation and well-being of the workforce.

Figure 7: Scenario 2: "Fusion of Private and Work Life".

1.2.3 Scenario 3: Living in a Bubble

What does a world look like in which robots and AI are boycotted by humanity and work and private life are integrated (Figure 8)?

- The world has stopped. Employees can structure their private and working lives flexibly and align them with their own needs.
- Workers are only marginally assisted by technological innovation, resulting in increased workloads.
- The boundaries between private and work life are blurring because employees have to be available at all times.
- Managers are faced with balancing high workloads and motivating employees.

Figure 8: Scenario 3: "Living in a Bubble".

1.2.4 Scenario 4: Back to the Old Days

What does a world look like in which robots and AI are boycotted by humanity and work and private life are strictly separated (Figure 9)?

- The world of work is returning to its roots. Low automation through robots and AI means that the lack of labor is faced with increasing demand.
- The strict separation between private and work life, coupled with fixed working hours, lead to less agility and slower processes.
- Executives are confronted with a lack of flexibility and capacity bottlenecks.

Regardless to which scenario might actually develop, these scenarios underline the challenges leadership is facing. And of course, one needs to point out that these scenarios are focusing on the future challenges in the context of work in an organization. Further challenges will arise due to the future dynamics of the respective industry an organization is operating in.

But let us consider some of the challenges arising from these scenarios for leadership. For one, leaders need to make sure that employees have the right skills to thrive in such an environment, but leaders will also be the one that need to determine what the relevant future skills are. Further, it will be challenging to establish a sense of community among a team, for instance, which is spread around the world, or which is frightened by the possible role AI can play in the

Figure 9: Scenario 4: "Back to the Old Days".

future. If private and work life merge stronger in the future, leaders will be challenged to not only be aware of this but also to lead differently.

Looking at these scenarios and considering how industries will change in the future and what this implies for organization, in particular in respect to change and transformation, it is paramount for us to answer the questions of how leaders can provide orientation in this situation. *What* do they want to achieve and *how* do they want to achieve this.

1.3 The Robust Leadership Framework

The robust leadership framework provides orientation in terms of *what* shall be achieved and *how* this *what* shall be achieved. While we will describe later in more detail the elements of the *what* and *how*, Figure 10 provides an overview. The *what* in our framework centers on strategy and foresight. Putting at the center the idea that, in particular in VUCA environments, leaders need to provide a long-term orientation on where the organization is heading. And providing a long-term orientation is very much about developing foresight, meaning imagining how the future could be, sensing changes in the environment but also challenging taken-for-granted assumptions and eventually transferring these insights into a strategy.

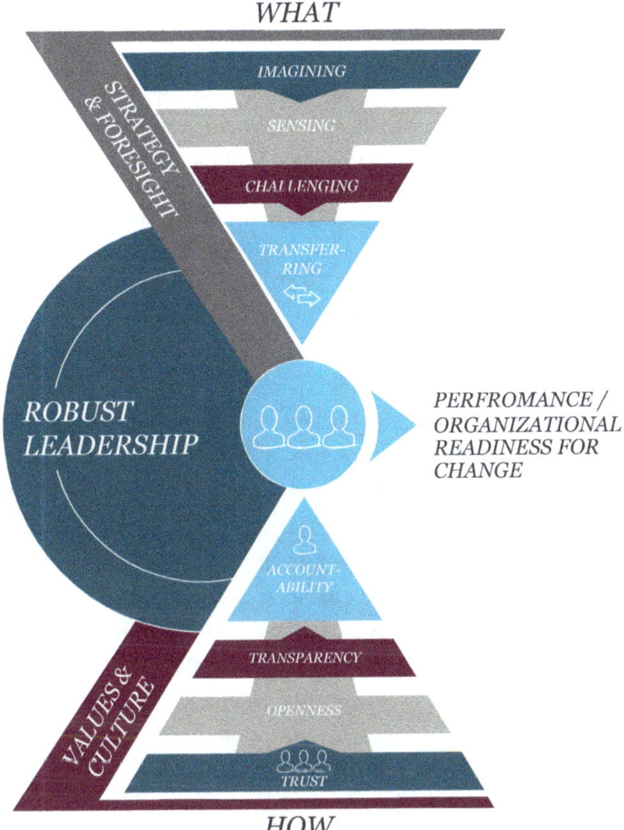

Figure 10: The robust leadership framework in detail.

Our main assumption for this framework is that in fast-changing VUCA environments, any initiatives in regard to foresight, strategy, or innovation inevitable lead to change and transformation. And therefore, the *how* is so relevant. *How* do we need to work together in organization to embrace the *what*, the new opportunities that are arising, and not just the challenges?

Why do we believe that "providing orientation" is so relevant for leadership in a VUCA world? General books on leadership, the kind you find in airport bookstores, are really about the inspirational leader. Simon Sinek's best-selling *Start with Why: How Great Leaders Inspire Everyone to Take Action* (2011), for instance, focuses on inspiration.

Jeffrey Pfeffer stated in an interview:

> The idea that leadership training is about inspiration strikes me as ridiculous. We know a lot about how to change behaviors on a sustained, successful basis – and inspiration is not the way. This neglect of evidence distinguished management from medicine and, for that matter, from any other field that has made progress over the years. (Schawbel 2015)

Others argue that influence is the essence of leadership, and that effective leaders need to influence others to carry out tasks. And that influence, especially in larger organizations, is based on power (Yukl and Gardner 2020). Acknowledging the role of power and formal or informal hierarchies in organizations, we also need to consider the dysfunctionalities of leading by power and influence which for instance is reflected in the high rate of disengagement among members of an organization. As we will also discuss later, our principle of providing orientation centers on the idea of engaging members of an organization into discussions or decision-making process, by for instance referring to open formats, and hereby not only creating buy-in or engagement but also providing orientation in terms of *what* shall be achieved and *how*.

If we put our approach of providing orientation in the context of proactive influence tactics (rational persuasion, inspirational appeal, consultation, collaboration, apprising, ingratiation exchange, personal appeal, coalition tactic, legitimating tactic, and pressure) within leadership research (Yukl and Gardner 2020), our approach comes the closest to collaboration. However, we do not refer here to collaboration as it would be described in a textbook on leadership: as an offer of a leader to help carry out a request. Rather, it is more about collaborating on eye level across hierarchies and organizational units to reach a goal.

While we will discuss leadership tensions (linear vs. stable, culture vs. strategy, authenticity vs. conformity and trust vs. guidelines) later, *striking a balance* is a key principle of leadership in a VUCA world. Based on our research on robust leadership, and especially on our work with numerous organizations, striking that balance is paramount in VUCA environments. This has been emphasized in the past in studies of ambidextrous organizations that, for instance, need to balance cost reduction with growing innovation activities.

The dynamics in the organizational environment underline that conventional either/or thinking is no longer appropriate. We cannot assume that there is only one perspective on changing circumstances and that leaders must balance all of them while being able to make decisions and arrive at conclusions.

Another guiding principle of our work is *understanding vs. consuming*. Leaders need to make sure that they and their teams do more than just consume information. They need to initiate discussions to create a common understanding of, for example, what relevance trends are, what they mean, and what they could imply. This entails a discussion of organizational values. A prerequisite is a *how* that supports such discussions along the lines of having a culture characterized by trust, openness, transparency, feedback, and development and accountability.

We witnessed such a situation when working with a regional bank on the values of their organization and the future of their industry. After several workshops, one executive felt comfortable enough to disclose that he actually did not understand one of the most important technological trends driving the future of his industry. Being so candid in this workshop about his own lack of knowledge was facilitated through a series of group workshops and discussions on *how* they want to work together as a leadership team. Creating a trusting atmosphere in the leadership team enabled the openness that made it possible for the team to move on with their discussions.

1.4 Effectiveness of the Robust Leadership Framework

Based on our two studies on robust leadership, we can analyze not only how our *what* and *how* of the robust leadership framework are related to each other but also how they contribute to distinct success measures.

In both studies, we find confirmation of the hierarchical structure of our pyramid, the *how*, in our framework. This means that trust is the basis for openness, transparency, feedback, and accountability. The existence of a trusting culture in an organization therefore is an enabler of, or a prerequisite for, the other items in our value pyramid.

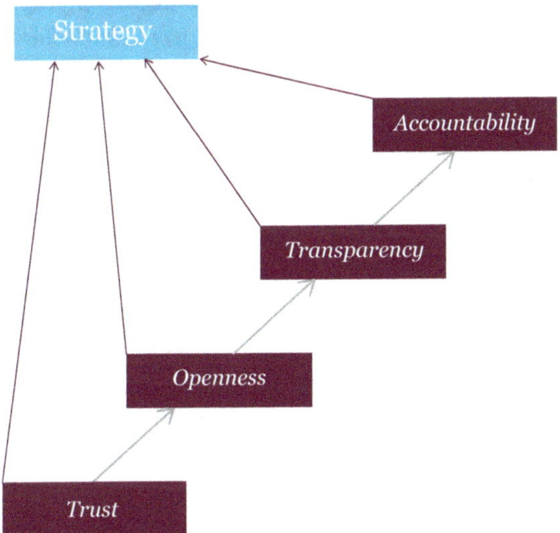

Figure 11: Interrelationship of *what* and *how*.

What our study shows (Figure 11) is that if the *how* is in place, it has positive effects on the *what*: strategy and foresight. This is a central finding because it underlines that strategy and culture need to go hand in hand. If trust is strong in an organization, that organization has the basis for developing foresight and strategy. And this makes sense. If my organization has a trusting culture, it is much easier for me to have discussions about the following issues: What are the major challenges in our environment? Do we all have a common understanding on what they mean? What does it mean for us? Do we need to challenge our assumptions concerning our industry, or how it works? What are the preferences of our customers? A closer look at our data makes this interrelationship even more apparent. If trust leads to openness, then based on our empirical investigation, trust and openness have a strong direct effect on the development of foresight and strategy.

In our empirical investigation, we also wanted to understand the role of values in the development of foresight and strategy. This speaks to our belief that the development of foresight and strategy is intertwined with the culture of an organization. And for us, the culture of an organization is reflected by its values and of course how the organization handles its values. Does it have values? Are they explicit? Does the organization live its values? We therefore asked the participants in our study if the leaders in their organization understand the relevance of values for organizational strategy. We found that in organizations whose leaders embraced the relevance of values, we see a stronger effect of the pyramid on foresight and strategy development, which again strengthens our belief that strategy and culture, the *what* and the *how*, need to go hand in hand.

Academic researchers (Leinwand and Mainardi, 2016) have argued that culture bridges the gap between strategy formulation and strategy execution which, in light of Peter Drucker's famous quote, "Culture eats strategy for breakfast," is not a surprise. However, they mention that the companies they researched, such as Starbucks, Danaher, or IKEA, which seem to be doing very well in reconciling strategy formulation and strategy execution, have high levels of trust.

Key takeaways from this chapter:

- Organizations face an increasingly complex and dynamic environment characterized by discontinuities and an uncertain future.
- The robust leadership framework looks at what it means to be an effective leader in such an environment and what mechanisms can help leaders to become effective.
- Robustness goes beyond resilience: perceiving change as an opportunity and harnessing it for the benefit of the organization. At the same time, it is about striking a balance between adapting to change and ensuring the stability of the organization.
- At the heart of the robust leadership framework is guidance on the questions of *what* an organization wants to achieve (strategy and foresight) and *how* (values and organizational culture).
- This involves two central principles: maintaining balance and providing orientation.

---

2 Tensions in Leading in a VUCA Environment

Questions addressed in this chapter:

- What tensions characterize day-to-day management and must be addressed by leaders for themselves and their organization?
- How do I, as a leader, assess these areas of tension for my organization and for myself?
- How can these tensions be addressed in practice?

In our two studies on robust leadership, we collected rich material on perceived tensions in leadership. We used the feedback to gain a better understanding of key aspects of leadership and of the challenges organizations and leaders are facing, and to identify the main fields of tension that leaders need to work in.

These tensions typically represent particular dilemmas or problems that seem tough or if not impossible to solve. As these tensions often arise from imminent challenges that pose a significant threat to the organization, they reveal weaknesses that are less obvious in day-to-day business.

In VUCA conditions, leaders face high levels of ambiguity, characterized by a lack of clarity and difficulty of interpreting a situation that presents with contradictory evidence. Ambiguity and contradictions might force leaders to act in areas of tension. These tensions then have the potential to create stress and create uncertainty in leaders about what behaviors they should demonstrate (Jordan, Wade, and Teracino 2020).

Conventional "either/or" thinking creates false dichotomies: for example, people must be either rational or creative and organizations must either optimize or innovate and be either sustainable or profitable. Leaders often think that different options are mutually exclusive, whereas in fact, it is often possible to combine different options. In *Competing for the Future*, Gary Hamel and C. K. Prahalad (1994) claimed that firms need to optimize their business while developing foresight and innovating their portfolio. Others have argued that leaders in a VUCA environment must combine a command-and-control style of leadership with a focus on participation and listening (Jordan, Wade, and Teracino 2020). Leaders who think strictly in "either/or" terms set up false contradictions. Ambidextrous leaders are better prepared for the challenges of a VUCA world, as they can reconcile and even embrace several contradictions at the same time.

These can appear at the levels of individual and organizational leadership. However, organizational tensions that arise from the structure of the organization or that are triggered by organizational changes often have a direct effect on leaders and thus reflect leadership tensions.

 | https://doi.org/10.1515/9783112242803-002

In the following, we describe two organizational and two leadership tensions (Figure 12).

Organizational Tensions:
- Linear and stable versus agile organizations
- Culture versus strategy/what? versus how?

Leadership Tensions:
- Authenticity versus conformity/me or the company?
- Trust and transparency versus guidelines

ORGANIZATIONAL

LINEAR & STABLE VS. AGILE

CULTURE VS. STRATEGY

LEADERSHIP

TRUST VS. GUIDELINES

AUTHENTICITY VS. CONFORMITY

Figure 12: Overview of leadership tensions.

We are now going to discuss these four tensions in more detail, starting with the organizational tensions. Besides describing the tension, we will cite some observations from our robust leadership studies, highlighting how leaders and organizations perceive and engage these tensions.

After describing each tension, we will offer a reflection exercise you can use to locate your organization and your leadership behavior and to express your thoughts. You can do these exercises by yourself and/or with your team. You can structure your thoughts on the template included with the exercise.

2.1 Linear and Stable Versus Agile Organization

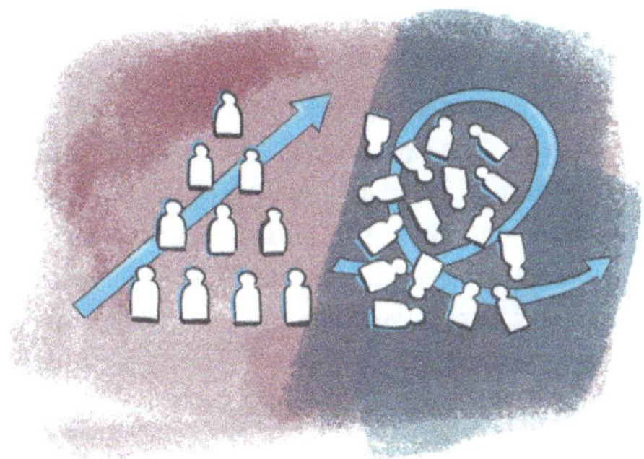

Figure 13: Leadership tensions: "linear versus stable".

Functioning organizations need stability, strategies, and long-term perspectives if they are to protect themselves and build on their previous successes. At the same time, however, organizations can keep up with their competitors only if they can react agilely to rapidly changing environmental conditions, have permeable structures, are creative and innovative, take risks and, if necessary, change plans, reverse decisions, and rethink strategies (Figure 13).

The ambidextrous organization (Birkinshaw and Gibson 2004) is one response to this tension. This form of organization consists of two parallel structures. One is quite stable and completes standard tasks; the other focuses on innovations and is therefore more flexible and agile. However, it is questionable whether such a clear separation works in practice or if it is more a matter of finding a balance.

This tension also affects leaders. How can they provide orientation and clarity while being change agents at the same time? Do they present themselves as constants or as agile adapters? Do they stick to decisions and thus convey reliability and security, or do they quickly adapt their decisions to changing conditions and sometimes risk triggering insecurity in the team or appearing arbitrary?

A few quotes from participants in our two studies make it clear how this tension shapes leadership in daily practice:

> *Very few people are equally strong in creative and strategic thinking, normally it is either/or.*
>
> *In German tech companies there is a gap between the culture within business units (KPI-driven, micro-management, etc.) and more explorative departments (corporate innovation, venturing, etc.) which is in the nature of the respective job. The question is: Where is the common ground of a cultural behavior and which common ground can both parties agree on?*

Example from Practice

The conflict between a clear perspective on the future and a high degree of adaptability is evident in many organizations.

Management's assumption about the level of information available to employees and managers is often incorrect. In the case of a pharmaceutical company, this became apparent during a management meeting. The CEO showed the steep growth curve the company was on, which as an exponential function stood in stark contrast to the company's previous development over the last 5 years. It quickly became clear that the management team was not fully aware of this context. Many changes in the company were based on the steep growth path. This generated an intensive discussion among those present and had a clarifying effect with regard to changes in the organization. It became clear that the tension between long-term growth and short-term measures was not sufficiently clear to everyone involved. For example, IT systems and processes were adapted in preparation for growth; this was perceived as a hindrance without the wider context, but formed the basis for further growth. The wider context had a clarifying effect on these adjustments and decisions in the organization. In retrospect, the managers described this insight as central.

The more agile and adaptable an organization is, the more important it becomes to accompany this with a long-term perspective and to communicate this sufficiently. The faster the adjustments are, the greater the employees' need for context and security. One manager described her experience as follows: "We are now very good at adapting our approach to the market in the short term and getting better. However, it is becoming increasingly challenging to communicate the rapid changes to employees and to keep them on board, as they often lack context. This is a big challenge for me in terms of communication and as a manager."

Reflection Exercise

This reflection exercise will situate your organization and your own leadership behavior within this field of tension. You can also express your thoughts on the tension. You can do this as an individual exercise and/or with your team.

Locate yourself on the scale and write down a few thoughts. If you are doing this exercise with your team or colleagues, give everybody some time for reflection and then share insights together or in small groups.

REFLECTION EXERCISE: Linear & Stable vs. Agile

Organisational field of tension

Is my organisation more focused on security, stability and linear processes or on renewal, innovation and agile processes?

Linear & Stable
Agile

Reflection: Which focus is more likely to be rewarded or recognised in the organisation?

What does this mean for my behaviour as a leader and what do I focus on? On providing security and maintaining the existing core business or on creating creativity, agile adaptation, risk-taking and innovation?

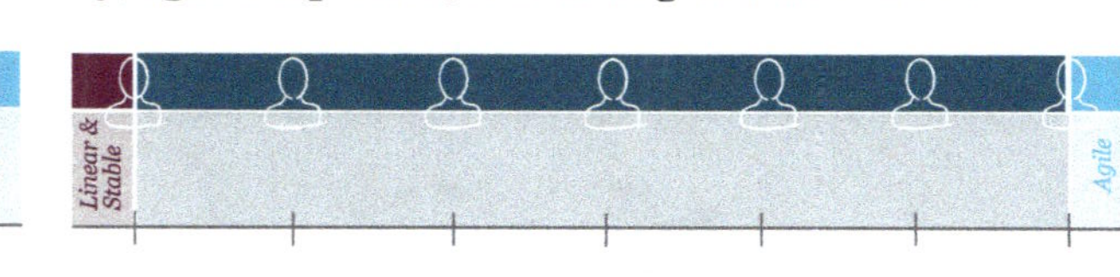

Reflection: Do I perceive tensions here? What challenges does this entail?

2.2 Culture Versus Strategy/What? Versus How?

Figure 14: Leadership tensions: "culture versus strategy".

We all know Peter F. Drucker's line, "Culture eats strategy for breakfast," but is it really that simple? Of course, Drucker did not assume that strategy is not important for companies, but the statement implies an "either/or" that does not correspond to reality. Culture and strategy do not compete. For either of them to be effective, they must cohere. It is important to recognize and balance the tension between culture and strategy, instead of having a focus on one or the other (Figure 14).

Organizational culture is central to business success. Values, as a part of the company's culture, drive a sense of belonging, they create meaning, guide decision-making, and reduce uncertainty and complexity. At the same time, shaping organizational culture is a difficult endeavor and targeted changes to the organizational culture are challenging.

John P. Kotter (2012) claimed that for change to succeed, a clear vision of the future that is linked to appropriate strategies is important. However, following Kotter, this vision must correspond to the needs of different stakeholder groups and the company's culture. It is the task of leadership to commit those affected to the common goal by clearly communicating the direction of change. And the vision must not only be understood; everyone affected must believe in it. Only then will employees be able to contribute to achieving the goal on their own responsibility. At the same time, everyone involved is pursuing the same goal.

The success of organizations relies on thinking strategy and culture jointly, coordinating and intertwining the *what* and the *how*. A clear separation does not meet today's requirements for companies.

What does this mean for leaders? They experience this tension as a rising complexity of focus. For instance, a leader might ask how can I focus on the creation and adaptation of the strategic direction while working on its transfer and integration with my team?

Again, we have compiled a few quotes from our studies that underline our remarks:

> *Values are the bedrock of any organization. Making them explicit helps to reinforce them and create a common language and identity. Thus, they are supporting a sustainable performance over time.*

> *Is there enough space and time available to build trust? Understanding that trust is key to business success and that it accelerates people's performance is crucial.*

Example from Practice:
How can strategy development be made transparent?

An IT unit of an automotive group in Germany: The new division manager knew that the success of the strategy transfer was a key success factor. At the same time, the unit was perceived as slow and critical within the group. How was it possible to get the team on board and quickly transfer the strategy to the organization?

Compared to previous strategy processes, which were limited to very few participants and confidential, the discussions were moved to a workshop area that was very visible near the entrance of the building. Employees could see the workshop groups and observe them at work. For security reasons, the discussions could not be heard and no details could be seen, but the teams' work on the strategy and its transfer could be observed. Employees thus experienced a culture of participation and shaping the future together; this led to a stronger sense of ownership and a faster application of the strategy into work practice. At the same time, the values were emphasized as an important part of the strategy by the managers in the workshops and thus the cultural context of the strategy was discussed. The managers and teams concretized the values in behaviors that were important to them for the strategy transfer.

A workshop format was chosen for the transfer to the teams, in which the managers initially worked cross-functionally. This was intended to encourage exchange and promote a common understanding of the strategy in the discussion. In the next step, the managers repeated the format with their own employees, supporting each other in the process. The focus was on the teams' contribution to the strategic fields and the values in the collaboration that were important for success.

During the process, it was observed that confidence in the strategy and in the future increased and that employees' perception of their role as IT employees also changed. The self-image of IT employees changed from a service model to the role of a driving force. The open process provided the impetus to fill this new role in the group organization and also to drive forward the introduction of agility with great consistency.

Reflection Exercise

Use the following template to reflect on the role of this tension in your daily work life, individually or with your team. Where do you locate your organization? Where do you locate your own leadership behavior?

Locate yourself on the scale and write down a few thoughts. If you are doing this exercise with your team or colleagues, give everybody some time for reflection and then share insights together or in small groups.

REFLECTION EXERCISE: Culture vs. Strategy

Organisational field of tension

Is my organisation more strategy-driven or culture-driven?

What does this mean for my behaviour as a leader and what do I focus on? On creating and adapting the strategic direction and practical implementation or on cultural aspects such as cooperation, behaviour and values?

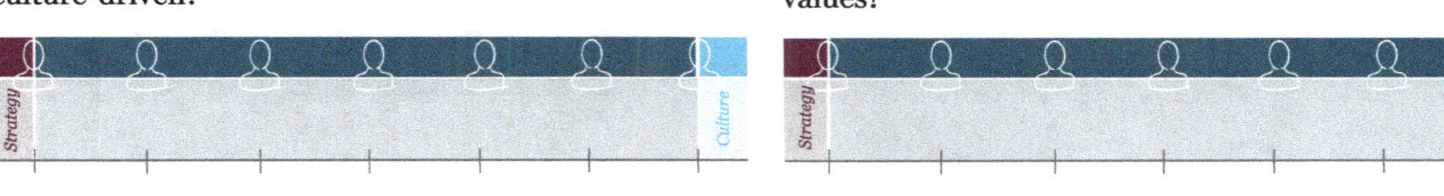

Reflection: Which focus is more likely to be rewarded or recognised in the organisation?

Reflection: Do I perceive tensions here? What challenges does this entail?

2.3 Authenticity Versus Conformity/Me or the Company?

Figure 15: Leadership tensions: "authenticity versus conformity".

How do I lead in conformity with the culture – the values, the norms, the self-understanding of the organization while being authentic at the same time (Figure 15)? An important part of the role of leaders is leading by example. This requires the leader's conformity with the values and goals of the organization. Leaders must act in the interests of the company and support its goals. This means to show and foster behaviors aligned with the company culture and goals. It is the responsibility of managers to provide guidance as to what is to be achieved and how it is to be achieved in a way that reconciles the interests of the company with those of the individual, thereby enhancing employee commitment.

To be successful role models, however, managers must also set an example of authenticity. Being authentic as a leader means being real, honest, sincere, and standing by your beliefs. Moreover, vulnerability is seen as a core aspect of contemporary leadership and an authentic leadership style (Brown 2018).

But what if authenticity and conformity become a conflict? Of course, companies check the cultural fit of new employees and leaders in the recruitment process, but that has its limits. And it becomes a problem, if the culture of the organization and the beliefs and values of the individual do not match. Either the individual manages adapt to the culture (over a longer period of time he or she can help to shape the existing culture), or the gap is so significant that it leads to the individual leaving the organization. This notion becomes particularly important in the context of the trend toward a more inclusive and diverse company culture which is generally perceived as an asset.

What does this mean for leaders? What happens, for example, if the culture in the organization changes over time and that no longer fits the values and beliefs of individual leaders? Or what happens if the management board releases a completely new personnel strategy or culture direction that questions the manager's learned self-image and values that were relevant before? This tension between conformity and authenticity can arise again and again, especially in times of rapid change and more diverse company cultures. As a leader, how do you resolve the resulting tensions? How can you strike a balance? What happens if you cannot strike that balance anymore?

This tension was mentioned by many participants of our studies. What follows are a few examples of how leaders experience this tension in their work:

> *To foster trust, a key leadership behavior is to show vulnerability. Unfortunately, not something that is understood nor demonstrated where I work.*

> *There is a discrepancy between what leaders say and what they really think.*

> *Credibility of leaders is based on authenticity and coherence (you do what you say). In middle size companies, distance is short and you get to know the behavior of the leader quite well. If values they talk about are not respected and put in practice, trust and further development of employees is possible.*

> *A high-performance team has unity of purpose that is aligned with their personal and group values.*

> *As a leader never ask your teams for something you wouldn't do yourself. Preaching water and drinking the wine yourself destroys the culture of the company.*

Example from Practice

A team leader, new to a long-established communications team at a German automotive group, encountered considerable resistance from the new team in his first few months at work, and his understanding of leadership did not seem to meet expectations. The team leader with significant leadership experience at an international level was accustomed to managing with a coaching attitude, allowing plenty of freedom, promoting personal responsibility, and supporting his own team. His team, in contrast, wanted clear announcements, a manager who would lead the way, stand up for the interests of the team within the group, and take disciplinary action for misconduct if necessary.

At the beginning of our consultation process, however, the needs landscape was rather cloudy. First and foremost, disputes within the team were the order of the day and a great deal of dissatisfaction was evident.

To clarify our understanding of the situation and to listen to the voices that were being drowned out by their more opinionated teammates, we first conducted individual interviews with every team member. In these interviews, their needs, fears, and assumptions became clearer. For example, it was revealed that the new boss's many freedoms, for instance, in regard to making decisions, were interpreted as a lack of interest.

A workshop on leadership culture in the team, in which the results of the interviews were discussed and a leadership model was collaboratively developed, was an important first step in narrowing the gap both within the team and between the team and management. However, the workshop also clarified the position of the manager. This open and trusting dialogue in a protected environment and with external, and therefore neutral, moderation led to regular, self-organized team meetings in which leadership and teamwork were reflected upon and, if necessary, improvement measures were developed.

Reflection Exercise

How closely do my own values, goals, and beliefs match those of my organization? To what extent do I personally feel a tension between conformity and authenticity? Where do I locate myself here? Use the following reflection exercise to collect your thoughts on this tension:

Locate yourself on the scale and write down a few thoughts. If you are doing this exercise with your team or colleagues, give everybody some time for reflection and then share the reflection either together or in small groups.

REFLECTION EXERCISE: Authenticity vs. Conformity

Leadership field of tension

Where do I place myself? Do I act and feel more in line with the values and goals of my company or do I concentrate primarily on acting authentically?

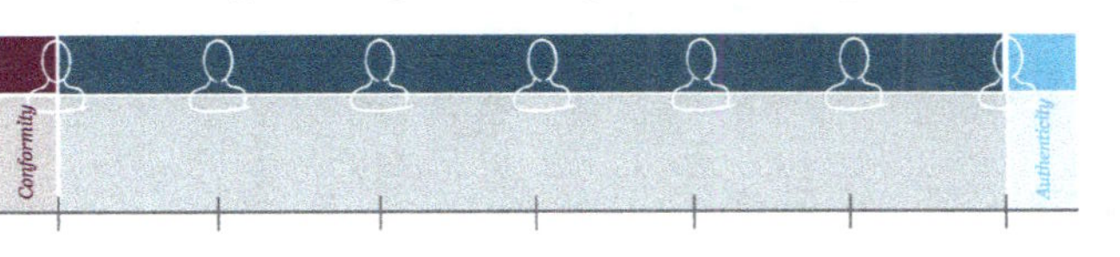

Reflection: How well do my own values, goals and convictions match those of my organisation?

Reflection: Do I perceive tensions here? What challenges does this entail?

2.4 Trust Versus Guidelines

Figure 16: Leadership tensions: "trust versus guidelines".

Trust plays a central role for organizations, but so does clear guidance from leaders. So how can a leader give trust and while setting guidelines or addressing performance without this coming across as distrust (Figure 16)?

In a highly dynamic corporate environment, a leap of faith can generate beneficial feedback, learning, and (personal) development and growth. The "trust must be earned" approach does not do justice to the pressure that a VUCA world puts on companies.

However, so that trust leads to the right results, and to ensure everyone is rowing in the same direction, the objectives must be clear. Leaders must provide orientation, a clear direction, and make the specifications to ensure coordinated collaboration. This is relevant, as a leader needs to be able to meet the requirements of their own superiors without weakening their own position by sharing power too broadly. Leaders must sometimes make quick decisions and act independently of their team. Performance management will never become obsolete in a culture of trust. So how can a leader give trust while setting guidelines? How can they encourage their teams to take responsibility and still make top-down decisions if needed? How can they improve performance without conveying a sense of distrust or a reliance on outdated hierarchical behavior?

This leads to a second facet of this tension: More trust is conducive to greater transparency in an organization. The greater the transparency in an organization, the easier it is for employees to take responsibility. But how much transparency is healthy?

Transparency can have a positive impact on a company. For example, transparency regarding strategies and responsibilities promotes employees' willingness to support the company's goals. But not every piece of information, consideration, and decision (immediately) made transparent by leaders might be helpful for a team. Too much transparency can have a negative effect, for example when confidential information is revealed, when changes are communicated before they have been sufficiently formulated or prepared.

What does this mean for leaders? Balancing trust in teams while ensuring the direction and performance in a company is a crucial challenge. Of course, this also means keeping team members motivated. In addition, it is often difficult for leaders to strike the right balance between too much and too little transparency. A middle way promotes a culture of transparency in which some information is kept confidential and some is not. The following questions are central: How can leaders support a culture of trust and ensure clarity about what a culture of trust means in day-to-day operations? And what is the right balance between too much transparency and not enough?

This area of tension becomes apparent in many of the answers given by the study participants:

> *Trust needs to be earned from both sides. For instance, can you argue with your leader with no consequences?*

> *Actively involve employees, share perspectives, give context, be open and honest, stand in for employees, respect them.*

Example from Practice:
The national subsidiary of a pharmaceutical company in Germany provided an example of how to deal with this area of tension.

After a restructuring, the new CEO realized the importance of building trust in the organization. Many employees were in crisis. Trust had been lost as a result of reorganization and employee morale was at rock bottom. This sentiment was reflected in the employee survey's engagement index. At the same time, the demands of the market and the global organization were increasing. The structure was also characterized by a high degree of centralization and strong micromanagement, both of which reflected the lack of trust in employee performance.

A core initiative to break this negative spiral was a culture program designed to strengthen confidence in the organization's abilities and its trust in employees and management. Greater autonomy turned out to be a lever for joint success.

Similar to the military principle of "Commanders intend," the focus was on the clarity of the desired target state within the framework of the culture program. If the objective is clear, a solution can be more freely developed. This principle of goal clarity should allow employees to find the best way to achieve it. This is especially important during crises, as long chains of command are too slow to react appropriately to a rapidly changing environment.

The principle of "Commanders intend" follows a process of "briefing and backbriefing." The manager discusses the goal with the employee, and then the employee goes back to the manager with a backbriefing of the goal and the planned solution. This helps the manager understand whether or not the employee has correctly understood the goal in the interest of the company. The process is repeated until the goal is achieved.

In the pharmaceutical company, the methodology and procedure were part of a train-the-trainer strategy and anchored in the teams as part of the working method. This made it possible to establish trust in practice and reduce micromanagement.

The effect of the cultural initiative led to a sharp increase in commitment within a year; the employees even exceeded their targets. At the same time, clear targets were balanced with practiced trust.

Reflection Exercise

We have prepared a reflection exercise for this last of the four tensions. How much trust do you give your team? How many guidelines do you set or do you have to set? How much does your team trust you to make the right decisions? How much transparency can you tolerate in your team? And as a manager, how much information do you (initially) have to keep to yourself?

Locate yourself on the scale and write down a few thoughts. If you are doing this exercise with your team or colleagues, give everybody some time for reflection and then share this reflection either all together or in small groups.

REFLECTION EXERCISE: *Trust vs. Guidelines*

Leadership field of tension

Do I concentrate primarily on strengthening trust in my team or on setting clear guidelines and and providing orientation?

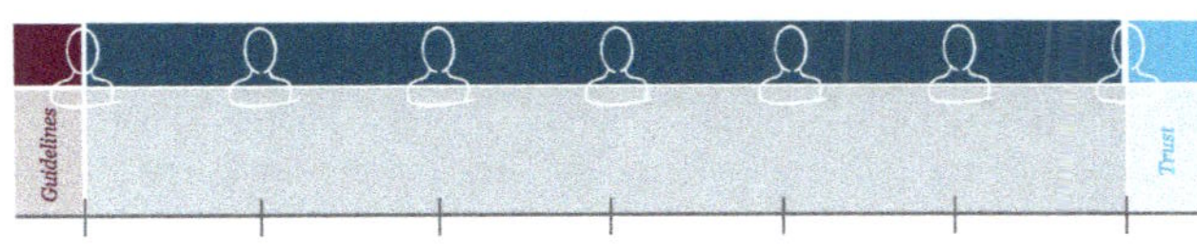

Reflection: What are the challenges for me in creating trust and security in my team and at the same time provide direction and orientation?

Reflection: Do I perceive tensions here? What challenges does this entail?

2.5 What to Make of These Tensions?

Where did you locate your organization and yourself within the four fields of tension? How do you experience these tensions? This form of reflection can help you to work on your leadership behavior and to find answers to different leadership situations.

In the following and final reflection exercise on the four tensions, you can reflect once more on how relevant the different tensions are for your daily work. Which area of tension should you take a closer look at because of the special challenges? Which areas of tension are less relevant in your everyday life right now, and can be temporarily put aside?

REFLECTION EXERCISE: Robust Leadership Areas of Tension

TRUST VS. GUIDELINES

How strongly do I perceive this tension in my day-to-day work?

NOT AT ALL | VERY STRONG

\+ , - . / 0 1 2 3 +4

AUTHENTICITY VS. CONFORMITY

How strongly do I perceive this tension in my day-to-day work?

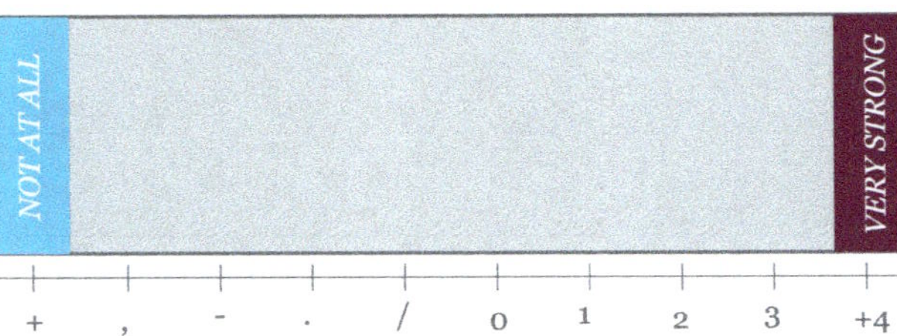

REFLECTION EXERCISE: Robust Leadership Areas of Tension

LINEAR & STABLE VS. AGILE

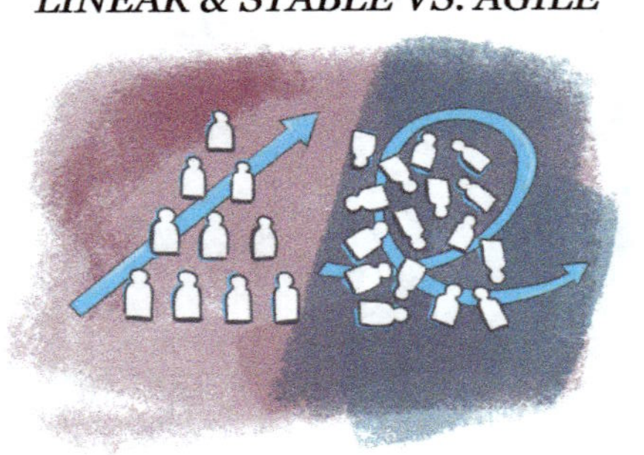

How strongly do I perceive this tension in my day-to-day work?

NOT AT ALL — VERY STRONG

\+ , - . / 0 1 2 3 +4

CULTURE VS. STRATEGY

How strongly do I perceive this tension in my day-to-day work?

NOT AT ALL — VERY STRONG

\+ , - . / 0 1 2 3 +4

Key takeaways from this chapter:

- There is no "either/or" when it comes to managing people and organizations. The leadership task lies in the ambidexterity of balancing tension and finding the right balance.
- We have identified four predominant areas of tension for leadership in a dynamic environment (two organizational tensions and two leadership tensions):
- The tension between the stable and agile organization; an area where leaders must balance the need for stability and direction of the organization while being agile in responding to or initiating change in the environment and within the organization.
- The tension between culture and strategy, in which managers must develop a balanced focus on both poles. This tension is even more about bringing strategy and cultural work together.
- The tension between authenticity and conformity arises when managers are expected to act as authentic role models and at the same time are in conflict with the values, procedures and goals of the organization.
- The tension between trust and guidelines reflects the challenge of conveying a high level of trust and transparency as a manager, promoting a culture of learning and feedback in the organization, while providing orientation through guidelines and specifications, addressing performance and making top-down decisions when necessary.

3 The Robust Leadership Framework: What?

Questions addressed in this chapter:

- What is the *what* in the robust leadership framework?
- Why is developing foresight central in a VUCA world?
- How does developing foresight link to strategy and the robust leadership framework?

A few insights from our robust leadership study:
Leaders at our organization . . .:

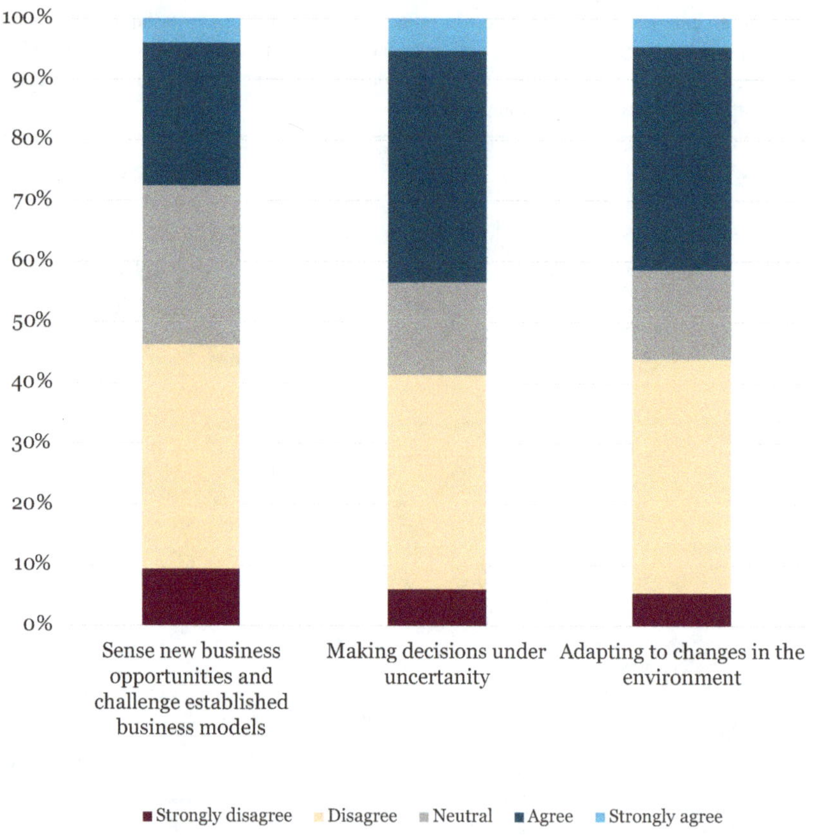

Figure 17: Insights from the robust leadership study.

 | https://doi.org/10.1515/9783112242803-003

Key takeaways:
- Most leaders are not good at sensing new business opportunities or challenging established mental models.
- This implies that most leaders find it difficult to prove orientation in a VUCA environment and to make sense of the changes in their industry.
- Further, most leaders find it difficult to make decisions under uncertainty or to adapt to changes in their industry.

We will now discuss one of the two central elements of our framework: the *what,* which means *foresight and strategy*.

If leaders need to provide orientation, this is achieved through proving orientation on *what* the organizations wants to achieve. Foresight is paramount to identifying this *what*. Foresight is twofold. First, it consists of exploring what is changing in an organization's environment through the detection of weak signals and trends. Second, foresight is not about making predictions but rather about understanding what alternative pictures of the future could be possible (Schwarz 2023). Developing foresight puts a leader and an organization in the position not only of being aware of the possible path of their industry's development but also provides a framework from which an organization may choose which future is desirable. And this allows for the formulation of a meaningful vision. The strategy, then, is the plan that enables an organization to make this vision a reality.

The element of the *what* – imagining, sensing, challenging, and transferring – all relate to what has been described as a corporate foresight:

> Corporate foresight is identifying, observing and interpreting factors that induce change, determining possible organization-specific implications, and triggering appropriate organizational responses. Corporate foresight involves multiple stakeholders and creates value through providing access to critical resources ahead of competition, preparing the organization for change, and permitting the organization to steer proactively toward a desired future. (Rohrbeck, Battistella, and Huizingh 2015: 2)

This definition has the advantage of focusing not only on perceiving changes in the business environment, in the form of weak signals and trends, but also on perceiving the relevance of deciphering how these changes might develop into the future and how organizations need to change in response to the insights derived from perceiving and prospecting.

Further, we perceive foresight as an activity which is predominantly geared toward the long term. We therefore emphasize the following definition: "Strategy is the direction and scope of an organization over the long term, which achieves advantage in a changing environment through its configuration of resources and competences with the aim of fulfilling stakeholder expectations" (Johnson, Scholes, and Whittington 2006: 3).

Focusing on the individual leader, the *what* is strongly related to strategic thinking. In other words, strategic thinking enables the development of foresight at an individual level. It is a leader's job to imagine how the organization's future can be different, to challenge assumptions about how to do business or how the industry operates, and to consider new ways of going forward. In making insights and assumptions explicit, leaders define the organization's vision and tangible goals. This is essential for strategy-making. It also drives innovation and enables organizations to keep adapting to an ever-changing environment.

We are aware of the term "strategic leadership" (Yukl and Gardner 2020). It reflects the way in which leaders can transform their companies to cope with constantly changing business environments. However, we want to make the context of the robust leadership framework more specific. This discussion also helps us to better understand how leaders can provide orientation in a VUCA world.

It has been argued that top executives must be sensitive to a wide range of events and trends in their organizational environment, all of which have the potential to affect their organization. Day and Schoemaker (2019) put foresight at the center of what they call *vigilant leadership*, as a way for leadership teams to manage the increasing turbulence in the business environment.

In the context of the COVID-19 pandemic, Paul Schoemaker (2020) of the Wharton School of Business underlines the relevance of strategic leadership. He suggests that during crises, leaders should ask questions like: What are the biggest uncertainties on the horizon? What scenarios should management develop to capture them? What strategic moves can the firm make to emerge as an industry leader? How robust are these moves across the possible scenarios? Clearly, here the link to developing foresight is made, also with the emphasis on perceiving turbulence, as in such crises, as an opportunity.

Further, leaders and organizations that engage in activities such as scenario planning are preparing their organization to respond well to crises, adding to the dynamic capability of that organization. Previous research has argued that developing foresight on an individual (leadership) and organizational level can be perceived as a microfoundation of dynamic capabilities (Schwarz, Rohrbeck, and Wach 2020). We also find evidence of arguments in the light of the COVID-19 pandemic, that it is essential to take a long-term view by applying foresight (Renjen 2020; Scoblic 2020; Krupp 2020). For us, questions such as "what is our vision?," "what is our north star?," or "what is our why?" are answered by the strategy and foresight component of our robust leadership framework.

In leadership theory, one will find the argument that when extreme events arise, the expectations of a leader change. During crises, leaders will be expected to be more assertive, directive, and decisive (Yukl and Gardner 2020). However, by labeling the current environment of an organization as VUCA, it appears that crises, for instance, are becoming "normal" in organizational environments; this indicates that a crisis mode is not a sufficient response to these kinds of organizational environments. While it may be counterintuitive, our position is that a leadership style in a VUCA world should be less about being assertive, directive, and decisive, and more about being collaborative, open, and transparent.

If we relate our robust leadership framework to leadership theory, it can be argued that robust leadership is a form of participative leadership. Participative leadership allows for others to participate in leaders' decision making. Other terms used in this respect are *joint decision-making, power-sharing, decentralization, empowerment, and democratic management* (Yukl and Gardner 2020). The following benefits can arguably be achieved: higher decision quality, higher acceptance of decisions by participants, more satisfaction with the decision-making process, and more developed decision-making skills.

A study by executive search firm Russell Reynolds Associates concluded that the attributes differentiating CEOs from others fall into three categories (Stamoulis and Mannion 2012):
1. Forward Thinking: the ability to plan for the future
2. Intrepid: the ability to perform effectively in complex and difficult environments
3. Team Building: the ability to achieve success through others

Again, we see here the necessity to address both elements (*what* and *how*) of the robust leadership framework. Robust leaders need to be capable of providing a clear orientation to the organization and to promote its strategy and values at the same time. In other words, leaders need to share explicitly and clearly with their organization's members *what* the organization wants to achieve and *how* to achieve this on the basis of which values, practices, and strategy.

What also becomes obvious at this point is that *how* people work together in an organization is essential in many elements of the *what*. For instance, to challenge assumptions, a leadership team requires trust and transparency.

Besides describing the elements of the *what* of our robust leadership framework on an individual level (Figure 18), we will be offering a set of reflection questions for each element. These questions are part of our robust leadership assessment tool which will allow you to assess the robustness of your leadership style and organization.

3.1 Imagining

Imagining is the capability of a leader to think about how the industry could be different, how customers could be different, or how the organization could be dif-

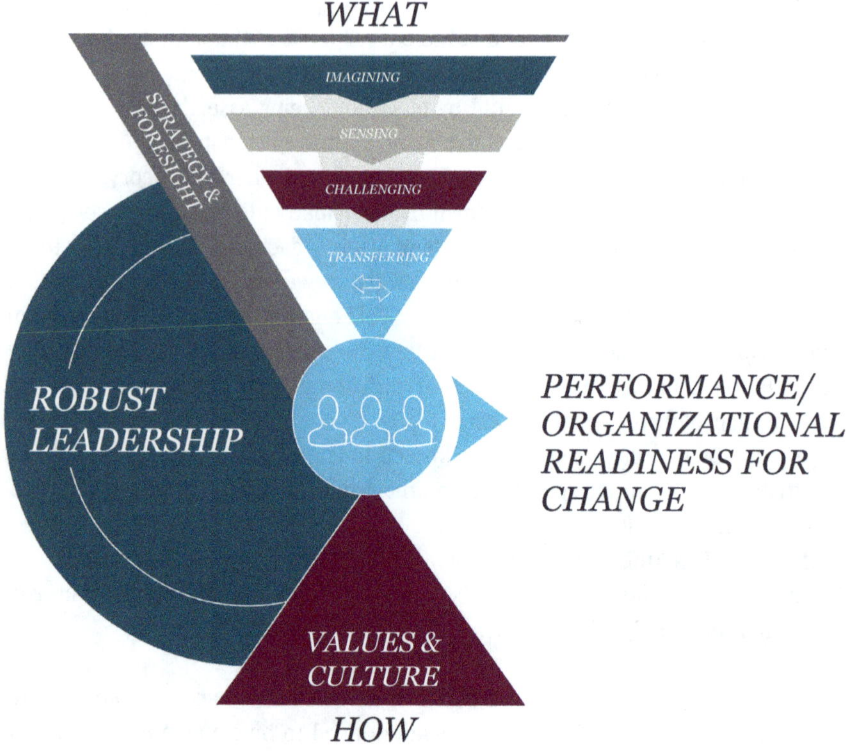

Figure 18: Robust leadership framework: What?.

ferent. It is the ability to imagine a vision for the company and provide orientation and stability going forward.

We still find in many organizations the assumption that past success will continue into the future. Dealing with many changes might therefore be more a question of gradual adaptation or incremental innovation. However, it is hard, especially for established organizations, to imagine the future differently from the past. Here again, strategic thinking is central to applying the tools we know from strategic foresight, like scenario planning. Again, we can see the link to culture and values, the *how* in our framework. A trusting, open, and transparent organizational culture supports these kinds of considerations.

A robust leader needs to be able to provide orientation by being able to imagine how the future could be like, how it could be different, how the industry could change, or how customer preferences could change. This power of imagination is a starting point for being a robust leader because of its inherent flexibility.

If one is not set on one course of action or one future, one might become more flexible in adapting to new circumstances and recognizing new opportunities.

But how can one foster the capability of imagination? For us, it is central to be clear that we cannot predict *the* future and that there is no such thing. The future is open. We need to think about multiple futures. In this way, we can open up and start imagining different futures.

One way to foster the capability of imagination is to read fiction. It has been argued that fiction can have positive effects on leaders. Stillmann (2017) describes the benefits:

1. Enhanced reasoning skills
2. Understanding complex problems
3. Increased empathy
4. Stress relief
5. Strong role models

But foremost, reading fiction and especially science fiction is a way to imagine how the future could be different and to challenge the own assumptions and beliefs about it (Schwarz and Hofmann 2019).

Large multinationals have for instance used science fiction novels and movies to think about the future implications of artificial intelligence (AI). These considerations and perspectives supported the organization in developing ethical guidelines for the application of AI. Car manufacturer Audi (Schwarz and Hofmann 2019) reportedly analyzed science fiction to imagine the future of mobility.

3.2 Sensing

Sensing is the ability not only to sense changes in the business environment, from weak signals and trends, but also to develop ideas how they could evolve, what future scenarios could be. This pertains to *imaging*. Sensing is a key capability to stay close to the developments in environment and to be adapt proactively. Thus, change is perceived as an opportunity, not as a challenge.

Rob-Jan de Jong (2015) establishes a strong connection between leadership and anticipation, or sensing. He argues that to grow their visionary capacities, leaders should develop their ability to see things early. Paul Schoemaker and George Day (2006) have called this the capacity to develop peripheral vision. It is important to see the small signals or weak signals of change that could develop into strong signals or trends over time.

Rob-Jan de Jong (2015) argues that leaders need to develop the ability to connect the dots, meaning to be able to create a picture, or several, of how emerging trends can play out in the future and how they are connected. The prerequisite for thinking about the future, however, is to acknowledge that we cannot predict the future. And as the future cannot be predicted and is not predetermined, we need to talk correctly about *futures* (Schwarz 2023).

Robust leaders need to be cautious about making simple predictions and must keep in mind that the future is open. They also need to keep what they are observing in a broad focus, perhaps not only trends within their industry but also trends in adjacent ones. Overall, robust leaders need to be capable of sensing business opportunities and risks before they fully materialize so that they can challenge the status quo, which bridges to the next element.

One way of achieving sensing capabilities is to pay deliberate attention to the non-mainstream, whether newsletters or conferences. This might include being open to conversations with different people. Diversity is the key element here, referring to a leadership team or the personal network. In the past, we have enjoyed what we called trend-safaris, taking executives on trips to let them experience subcultures or emerging technologies, thereby creating an awareness of what is happening on the periphery of their business.

3.3 Challenging

Challenging is probably the most difficult capability to develop as a leader or organization. It is the ability of creative destruction needed to adapt. It means to challenge assumptions on how the future could develop. It is the ability to unlearn things that have worked in the past but might not be helpful now or in the future. Many big corporations have excellent sensing capabilities in their strategy functions. If you sense a new development in your environment but you are not able to adapt your behavior, process, or business model to it, that insight is purely academic. To challenge is key to truly translating the input from the environment into the organization and then changing direction. This is how to seize an opportunity apparent in the environment or mitigate risks.

Leaders need to provide orientation to their organizations by being the ones that challenge common assumptions and unquestioned beliefs by providing new perspectives to the organization. In particular in VUCA environments, "old" assumptions might be dangerous, often rooted in an organization's past success. Strategic thinking is essential for a leader to be the one in the room who challenges. Further, if the leader is the challenger, this signals to the organization the relevance of this skill.

A robust leader must constantly be aware of the cognitive traps into which an organization is likely to fall. One of the authors had a fireside chat with the chief operating officer of an insurance company. One senior manager understood that products such as car insurance policies could be sold online. However, he was also convinced that life insurance products could not. Shocked, the chief operating officer replied: "Go to the website of one of our competitors and you will see how life insurance policies are sold online." What we can observe here is that no one had challenged this assumption. We can also get an idea of how assumptions that have long gone unchallenged can have a lasting impact on an organization.

This also implies that robust leaders need to be open, not only to new impulses from within their organization but to external impulses such as building and nurturing external networks.

3.4 Transferring

Transferring is the last identified capability. It means how good someone is at gaining traction once a new direction has been decided. How fast can you translate insight into action? It means changing a strategy and consequently an organization so that it can chart a new path. One could argue this is the part that turns an organization around.

For us, transferring means that a robust leader is in the position not only to imagine, sense, and challenge but also to move teams based on these insights that can be translated into action.

Steering the organization toward its goals is particularly important in a VUCA world. It presupposes that leaders are capable of generating understanding within their teams and throughout the organization. Change guru John P. Kotter argues that leaders overestimate the impact of communicating a vision. He argues that if leaders believe that their message is well perceived, they might need to repeat it 10 to 100 times (Kotter 2012). Therefore, a robust leader needs to be capable of both formulating and communicating a clear vision.

Further, for us, transferring implies that robust leaders are capable of transferring foresight insight into strategy and then into tangible projects.

3.5 Reflection Exercises

Please take a moment to reflect on the following questions. If you are doing this exercise with your team or colleagues, give everybody some time for reflection and then share this reflection either all together or in small groups.

REFLECTION EXERCISE: Imagining

Do you seldom or regularly imagine how your industry or organization could be different?

Do you read fiction or science-fiction?

Can you think of anything that supports you in imagining?

REFLECTION EXERCISE: Sensing

Are you actively also considering trends from the outside of your industry?

Are you thinking in multiple futures, or multiple scenarios, in respect to the future of your industry?

Are you actively seeking conversations which provide you with new and different perspectives?

REFLECTION EXERCISE: Challenging

Are you actively challenging your own assumptions?

Are you challenging the assumptions within your team or organization?

Have you created or experienced an atmosphere in your organizations that fosters challenging assumptions?

REFLECTION EXERCISE: Transferring

Has your organization formulated a clear vision and has that vision been sufficiently communicated?

Has your vision been broken down your to unit to your team?

Do you translate strategy into concrete projects?

Key takeaways from this chapter:
- In VUCA environments, it is essential for leaders to provide orientation by developing a long-term perspective, being aware of changes in the business environment, and developing foresight through alternative pictures of the future.
- Robust leaders need to exercise their imagining, sensing, challenging, and transferring capabilities.
- The *what* in the robust leadership framework already needs to reflect the how. In other words, the *how* in organization is an enabler for the *what*.

4 The Robust Leadership Framework: How?

Questions addressed in this chapter:

- What are the key capabilities on the cultural level that leaders and organizations need to thrive in an uncertain environment?
- Which aspects of leadership and culture move into the focus of the discussion?
- What is your individual situation as a leader?

A few insights from our robust leadership study:
Leaders at our organization . . . :

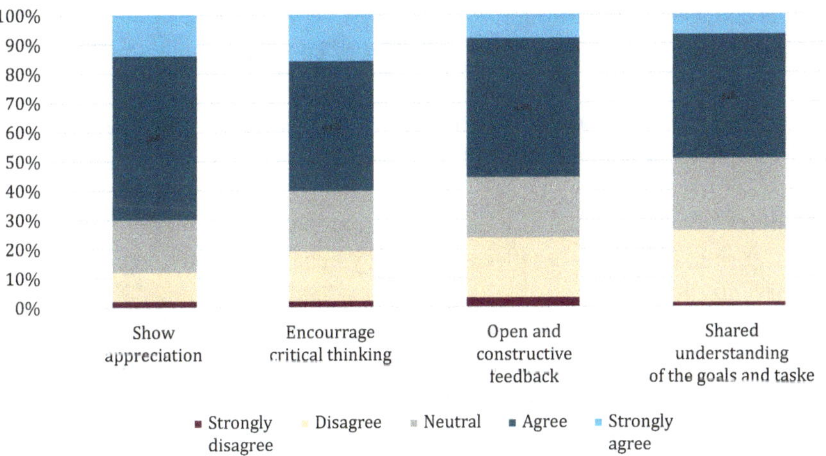

Figure 19: Insights from the robust leadership study.

Key takeaways:

- Considering these aspects from our study, it seems that leaders have better skills developed in the *how* of our framework than in the *what*.
- However, less developed is the skill to create a shared understanding of tasks and responsibilities, which indicates that accountability is less developed.
- It is remarkable that roughly two-thirds of leaders surveyed in our robust leadership study express their appreciation of work done by the team members, indicating that a trusting environment has been established.

Providing orientation in terms of the *what* is one element of our robust leadership framework. The other element is *how* the *what* shall be achieved. It is therefore essential for foresight, strategy, culture and values to go hand in hand. In other words, we need to make sure that culture doesn't eat strategy for breakfast

 | https://doi.org/10.1515/9783112242803-004

or vice versa. A strategy reflects the way in which the culture might support a course of action but also how that culture might need to be changed to support a strategy. Foresight and strategy, and culture and values are two sides of the same coin. They must be considered and balanced at the same time if an organization is to succeed in a VUCA world.

Every organizational vision, strategy, or innovation implies change. However, changing organizations is a difficult task. The "guru" of change management, John P. Kotter (2012), has reiterated that many change initiatives fail. At the same time, we are all aware of barriers to strategy implementation such as insufficient time for change or resistance to change from the members of an organization, either because they haven't understood the purpose of the change or because they do not see themselves as part of the change journey.

This has several implications:

(1) Strategy and consequently foresight need to be thought about together with change in the first place.
(2) Change always implies how the culture of an organization actually supports the implementation of a strategy.

The culture of an organization is something that you cannot place on display in the entrance hall. Culture is reflected by many behaviors, traditions, or artifacts in an organizational context.

Understanding or assessing an organizational culture is a difficult task. Edgar Schein (1992: 12) defined *organizational culture* as "a pattern of shared basic assumptions that the group learned as it solved its problems of external adaptation and internal integration, that has worked well enough to be considered valid and, therefore, to be taught to new members as the correct way to perceive, think, and feel in relation to those problems."

To make culture explicit in organization we have focused in our consulting work on values, stressing with our clients the performance relevance of values. Brian Chesky, CEO of Airbnb, said: "Culture is a thousand things, a thousand times. It's about living the core values; when you hire someone, when you write an email, when you work on a project, when you walk down the hall. By living the values, we have the power to build a culture." What has worked well for us is to use values as proxy to understand the culture of an organization.

Leaders also need to provide orientation in terms of how the organization will achieve its goals. In other words, how do we need to work together to be successful? Why do we need to change and adapt? How an organization pursues its goals in practice relates to its values and how its members enact and experience them. Organizational values are essential for collaboration across hierarchical levels and functions and define the organization's culture.

Values are paramount in our robust leadership framework. We are concerned with how leaders provide orientation through their values. However, this implies that it is not sufficient for leaders to make general claims about "our common values"; it is about making values explicit by discussing them, especially what they mean for each individual and team. It is also about living and measuring those values.

When we discuss values and their relevance for performance, we consider two effects:

1. Values, as part of our robust leadership framework, provide orientation in terms of how teams or organizations work together to achieve a goal.
2. Ethical behavior and values can also be perceived as how organizations or their leaders behave internally and externally.

Several years ago, one of the authors had a conversation with the head of HR of a globally leading insurance company. The manager described the organization's work on values: "When somebody asks me about our values, I pull out my wallet. And in my wallet, I have a card on which our values are stated." Although at least this organization had its values written down, we would describe this situation as missed opportunity for leadership to use values as a means of orientation.

We find several references that reinforce our view on the relevance of values for leadership. Kim Scott (2019) uses "Radical Candor" to emphasize the relevance of leaders to build relationships, with their teams. Establishing trust is a core competence that permits not only open, direct, and constructive feedback but also accountability. We also find that competent leaders are able to generate high levels of trust, engagement, and productivity, but the actions of incompetent leaders result in members of an organization becoming anxious and alienated (Chamorro-Premuzic 2020).

Our pyramid of values, as part of our robust leadership framework, includes individual, team, and organizational perspectives. It identifies critical capabilities for high-performance teams and organizations to perform in uncertain environments.

We flesh out the dynamic between the levels of the pyramid to provide an overview of our robust leadership framework in respect to the *how* (Figure 20).

Trust is important in a variety of dimensions. A culture's strengths reside in its values and how well they are enacted internally and externally through consistent behaviors, rituals, and actions. Trust builds on different factors on the team and organizational levels. Key parameters include the feeling of a team "being in it together," and the feeling of having one's individual impact appreciated.

On a team level, trust allows for openness. When we trust each other, we can share our perspectives, concerns, and viewpoints. This becomes very important

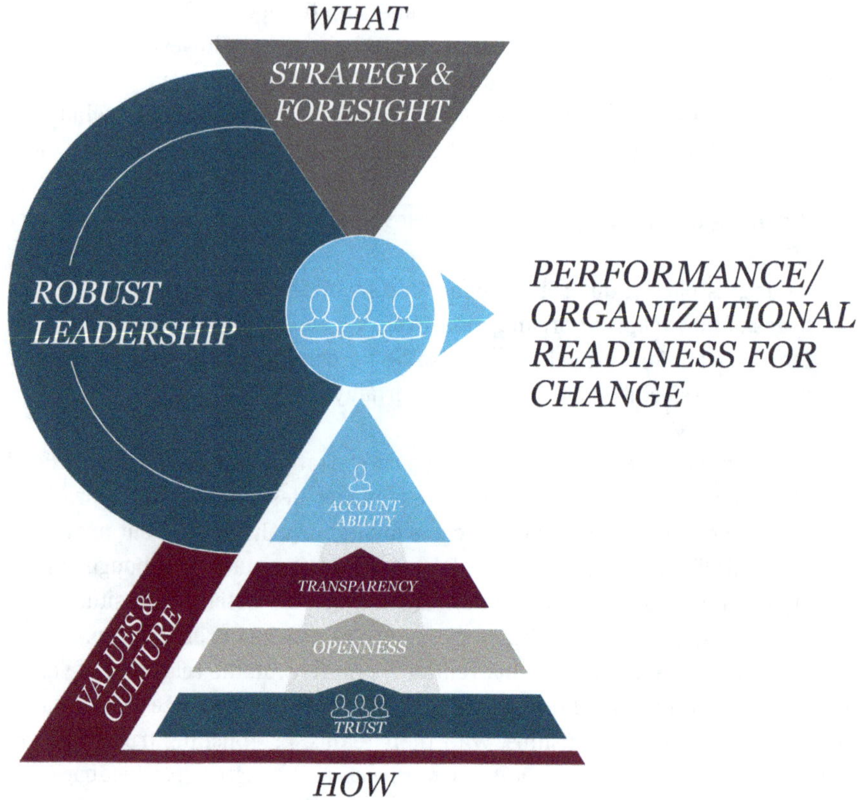

Figure 20: Robust leadership framework: How?

on both the team and organizational levels, because a diversity of perspectives is needed to perceive impulses from the business environment and for people to challenge themselves. If the culture of a company is conformist, its decisions might rely on redundant and filtered information. Therefore, changes in the business environment might be missed or even ignored. There is a strong impact of a culture allowing for openness in teams and diverse perspectives on the capabilities of perceiving and challenging in the upper triangle of the framework.

Trust and openness set the stage for a learning culture. Only if we trust each other, will we be able to provide transparency and give honest feedback. Missing out on transparency and feedback on the individual and team levels result in a lack of learning and development. As a leader from the automotive industry confirmed: "In our projects all traffic lights are green, people are too afraid of the consequence to report something else. Everybody knows the reality is different, but everybody participates in the game." Patrick Lencioni (2010) summarizes the effect in terms of artificial harmony, where conflicts are under the surface. On an organizational level, you will see how good an organization is at being transparent about its failures. If a company has ambitious goals and explores new terrain, failures will be part of the process. The likelihood of failures will increase in a dynamic and complex environment as part of the adaptation to new circumstances or the shift in a company's direction. Therefore, the learning culture is a key capability to develop.

In today's dynamic and rapidly changing business environment, organizations need to be adaptable to remain competitive. They must therefore develop a workforce that has the abilities, knowledge, and competencies to thrive in the workplace of the future (World Economic Forum 2020). How good is an organization in assessing and developing new skills needed in a changing environment? Again, this needs high levels of openness and trust in the organization to allow for the transparency needed. Future skills include a range of technical and nontechnical skills such as critical thinking, creativity, emotional intelligence, future, and digital literacy. Developing these skills within an organization is crucial for driving innovation, improving productivity, and enhancing organizational performance. By investing in future skills development, organizations can create a workforce that is equipped to handle the challenges of the future and drive success. Furthermore, employees are more likely to be engaged and motivated when they are given opportunities to learn new skills and develop the skills they already have.

Accountability, which is critical for performance, is at the top of the pyramid. Clear accountabilities allow the delegation of decisions and task to workers who possess the right skill sets. It counters micromanagement and with that slow decision processes and adaptations. Accountability is critical in dynamic environments that must adapt quickly.

To realize accountability, trust in employees is needed. Trust and accountability are the two sides of a coin. Accountability needs freedom in decision-making to solve a problem, perform a task, or create an impact. Not feeling accountable might lead to inattention to results and poor performance in an organization (Lencioni 2010). As Brene Brown (2018) points out in *Dare to Lead*, accountability encompasses the right to decide on the topic given and leaders must ensure that the skills are appropriate. Furthermore, accountability needs the trust in employees to succeed at a task.

Accountability is therefore a critical component of organizational performance, as it helps to ensure that individuals and teams take responsibility for their actions and decisions. When individuals are held accountable for their performance, they are more likely to take ownership of their work, strive for excellence, and make decisions that align with the organization's goals and values

(Gotsis and Grimani 2016). In addition to improving performance, accountability also helps to build trust within an organization. When individuals are held accountable for their actions, it demonstrates that the organization values honesty and integrity and is committed to treating everyone fairly and consistently. In conclusion, accountability is a key component of organizational performance, one that is essential for building trust, achieving goals, and protecting a reputation. Organizations that prioritize accountability are more likely to succeed in the long term.

The following sections examine each element of the *how* of our robust leadership framework, including guidance for leaders.

4.1 Trust

Trust is the base of our pyramid of values. As the foundation of the pyramid, everything rests on it, particularly with regard to accountability for actions and decisions.

Trust, an essential component of social interaction, is the belief that others will act in a way that is in our best interest. In organizational settings, trust is crucial in building relationships between individuals, teams, and the organization. It is also an indispensable element in the creation of a positive organizational culture, where employees feel safe, secure, and valued, and where collaboration and cooperation are encouraged (Dirks and Ferrin 2002).

Trust in organizations can be characterized as both cognitive and affective. Cognitive trust is the perception that others are competent, reliable, and well-intentioned; affective trust is based on emotional connections and feelings of warmth and affection (Mayer, Davis, and Schoorman 1995). Both cognitive and affective trust are important in building strong relationships and positive outcomes in organizations.

Trust is critical in shaping employee attitudes and behaviors toward their work and their organization. Research has shown that employees who trust their managers are more likely to exhibit positive work behaviors, such as increased commitment, job satisfaction, and organizational citizenship. Trust in leaders has also been found to be positively related to job performance.

Trust has a significant role in team dynamics and performance. Teams with high levels of trust are more likely to collaborate effectively, share information, and work toward common goals. Trust among team members can lead to improved decision-making, increased creativity, and better problem-solving abilities. Furthermore, trust in teams can enhance interpersonal relationships and result in greater job satisfaction and reduced turnover.

Trust also affects organizational performance. Organizations with high levels of trust are more likely to report increased productivity, greater innovation, and improved financial performance. Trust can also lead to improved customer satisfaction and loyalty, as customers prefer to do business with organizations they trust.

Trust is the basis of psychological safety, a concept that has gained considerable attention in the context of organizational behavior and team dynamics. *Psychological safety* is the extent to which individuals feel safe expressing themselves, sharing their ideas and opinions, and taking risks. Psychological safety has been identified as a key factor in promoting collaboration, creativity, and innovation, as well as in reducing stress and improving mental health.

For Frei and Morris (2020), trust is the essential building block of leadership, especially when the aim of leadership is to empower others. For them, building trust has three drivers: authenticity, logic, and empathy. *Authenticity* is when members of an organization perceive the interaction with a leader as "real." *Logic* is having faith in the judgment and competence of leader. *Empathy* means that a leader is perceived as caring about the members of his or her organization.

In *Humanocracy: Creating Organizations as Amazing as the People Inside Them*, Garry Hamel and Michele Zanini (2020) advocate rebuilding organizations from the bureaucratic obsession of control to an organization's maximizing human contribution, which they term *humanocracy*. Trust plays a vital role in humanocracy in the performance relevance of values.

Creating trust in an organization is very much about how leaders behave. For us, creating trust means making explicit that leaders trust their team members and that trust does not need to be earned over a long period of time. This can mean that leaders create an atmosphere in which failure is perceived as a valuable learning opportunity, not something for which employees will be penalized.

Creating trust in an organization also means that employees see their leaders show their appreciation for the work being done and for other initiatives. In addition, leaders create a strong identity of "being in this together" and protect their team. This might also include that leaders foster the sense of individual meaning and contribution to shared organizational goals.

4.2 Openness

For us, *openness* refers to the way we communicate, share our insights and concerns. Openness is central to having, for instance, discussions about emerging trends, the future, and of course what needs to change in an organization. In *Who Says Elephants Can't Dance?* Lou Gerstner (2003), the former CEO of IBM, describes IBM's transformation from a hardware producer to a solution provider.

When starting at IBM, he noticed that there was little discussion in meetings with the top executives. Gerstner later discovered that many executives had executive assistants who had prepared for many meetings by negotiating the outcome of decisions and pushing for compromises ahead of time, so that there would be no conflicts in the meetings. At IBM, this created a no-debate culture and the agreement to set a minimal standard or compromise. Lou Gerstner put a swift end to this system.

In VUCA environments, we need to challenge our assumptions, share our conflicting perspectives, and engage in open debates. To have these open debates, a culture of openness must be rooted in a culture of trust. In such a culture, members of the organization trust that they can express themselves and even disagree with the CEO without reprisals.

We strongly believe that in organizations challenged with a VUCA environment, openness is a key asset and of course the prerequisite for openness is trust. For us, openness in an organization starts with employees profiting from an atmosphere created by their leaders that promotes an open exchange of ideas, feelings, and concerns. This includes leaders who encourage critical thinking and raise challenging issues. Establishing simple brainstorming rules, such as don't criticize others, encourage wild ideas, stay focused, one conversation at a time, and build on the ideas of others (Brown 2009), can be very helpful in creating an atmosphere of openness in an organization.

What further supports an atmosphere of openness in an organization is that employees are encouraged by their leaders to communicate cross-functionally and cross-hierarchically. A robust leader can achieve this by living this principle by, for instance, exchanging on ideas or project cross-functional and cross-hierarchical themselves in the organization.

4.3 Transparency

Openness leads us to our next level of our pyramid: *transparency*. If we are transparent in regard to our tasks or goals, our concerns, our challenges, and of course our failures, we enable a *how* that is beneficial for organizations in a VUCA environment. With an increasingly dynamic and uncertain business environment, many companies are now under pressure to innovate more quickly. The claim "if you haven't failed, you have not tried" has become popular. However, this notion of failing is difficult for many companies to accept.

Picture the traditional German engineering company, very proud of making no or hardly any mistakes. Allowing for failure in innovation, while embracing perfectionism in production, is a difficult balance. However, transparency, enabled by openness and trust, is key here. The aim of transparency is, for instance, to make clear who is working on what, making the goals of the firm transparent, and how they link to the overall strategy. The Objectives and Key Results (OKRs) (Doerr and Page 2018), as a means to steer an organization toward a desired goal, were popular in the past. One of the OKR key principles is to achieve full transparency on the objectives of an organization and of course on the key results that need to be achieved to meet the objectives. This requires an organization to be in a position to deal with this kind of transparency.

Consequently, transparency is the basis for *feedback*, allowing an organization and its members to receive feedback. On the organizational level, a feedback culture is described by the company's learning culture. Learning culture is essential for organizations that want to remain competitive in today's rapidly changing business environment. By promoting continuous learning and development, organizations can improve employee engagement, retention, and performance, and create a more innovative and adaptable workforce. Research has shown that organizations with a strong learning culture tend to have higher levels of employee engagement, retention, and performance (Marsick and Watkins 2015).

Leadership is a key component of a learning culture. Leaders who prioritize and model learning and development can help to create a learning culture by supporting employee learning, creating opportunities for collaboration and knowledge sharing, and promoting a growth mindset (Denning 2018). Another component of a learning culture is the availability of learning resources. Organizations that give their employees a variety of learning resources, such as online courses, workshops, mentoring, and coaching, tend to foster a culture of continuous learning and development (Denning 2018).

Building on openness, to foster transparency and feedback, leaders need to provide context and orientation for decisions, goals, tasks, and responsibilities within their organization. While this can make transparency difficult for a leader, OKRs, for instance, are a way of making it clear who needs to contribute what to support an organization in reaching its goals.

4.4 Accountability

Finally, *accountability* builds on all of these elements. Leaders and employees should meet as equals and have trust in each other to fulfill their respective responsibilities. At the same time, leaders must ensure employees know their specific roles and responsibilities. Leaders can support accountability by reiterating a shared understanding of the goals and tasks (for instance, through briefing and backbriefing). They should also reemphasize *what* an organization must achieve, and *how*. However, achieving accountability can be difficult, particularly in large and complex organizations. Leaders must be committed to modeling accountability, and establish systems and processes that support accountability throughout the organization (Latham and Pinder 2005).

An organization can foster accountability through clear performance metrics, regular feedback and communication, and consequences for poor performance or misconduct. Organizations that prioritize accountability are more likely to achieve their goals, attract and retain top talent, and maintain a positive reputation.

An interesting approach, derived from the military, is "commander's intent." In addition to providing clarity and direction, this principle ensures accountability and maintaining situational awareness. By clearly communicating the mission and objectives, individuals and teams are better able to understand their roles and responsibilities and can be held accountable for their actions (Bungay 2011).

Accountability is essential in military operations where lives may be at stake. With "commander's intent," individuals and teams clearly understand the mission and objectives and are better able to take appropriate actions. This helps to ensure that everyone is working toward the same goal and that all actions are consistent with the mission.

Another key aspect of commander's intent is backbriefing, in which individuals and teams provide feedback to their superiors. Backbriefing helps to ensure that everyone is on the same page, and that there are no misunderstandings or miscommunications that could lead to mistakes. Furthermore, it informs a leader on the competence of the team members and if they have the skills to perform a task or solve a problem.

Backbriefing is an important aspect of accountability, as it ensures that individuals and teams are taking ownership of their roles and responsibilities and are actively engaged in the mission. By providing feedback and asking questions, individuals and teams demonstrate that they are fully aware of the mission and objectives and can take appropriate actions to achieve them.

Commander's intent is a powerful tool for aligning individuals and teams toward a common goal. It helps to provide clarity and direction, improve communication, reduce uncertainty and ambiguity, and increase efficiency and effectiveness.

4.5 Reflection Exercises

Please take a moment to reflect on the following questions. If you are doing this exercise with your team or colleagues, give everybody some time for reflection and then share this reflection either all together or in small groups.

REFLECTION EXERCISE: Trust

Do you feel trusted in your organization? Do you trust your employees?

Is trust one needs to earn in your organization?

Have you created an atmosphere of trust in your team or organization?

REFLECTION EXERCISE: Openness

Is there an atmosphere of openness in your organization?

Do you actively create an atmosphere of openness in discussions?

Do you show appreciation for critical thinking in your team?

REFLECTION EXERCISE: Transparency

Do you have transparency of the goals of the organization?

Have you made your goals as leader transparent to your team?

Are you providing and receiving constructive feedback?

REFLECTION EXERCISE: Accountability

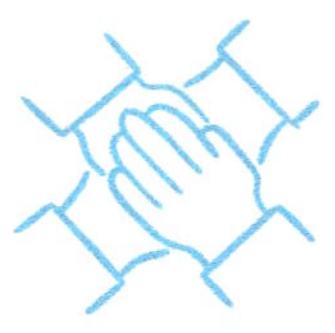

Have you created and shared understanding of goals and tasks in your team or organization?

Have you communicated for what you are accountable?

Have tried back briefing in your organization?

Key takeaways from this chapter:
- Trust, openness, transparency, and accountability are the elements of the *how* in our robust leadership framework.
- Trust is central, as it is the building block.
- Trust leads to openness, openness leads to transparency, and transparency leads to accountability.

---

5 Becoming a Robust Organization

Questions addressed in this chapter:
- How can an organization become **robust?**
- How can the individual perspective of the robust leader be linked to the robust organization?
- What are the ways to foster an organization's robustness?

We now discuss how the robust leadership framework can be applied on an organizational level. Two perspectives guide our discussion of our robust leadership framework: the organizational and the individual.

Of course, these two levels are intertwined and support each other. As with the *how* and the *what*, they are two sides of the same coin. In this chapter, we will focus on the organizational aspects.

We will highlight from our practice how robust leadership can be developed at the organizational level. Relating to our principles of robust leadership, we will emphasize the relevance of participation and engagement to balance the *what* and the *how*. We will then introduce the Institute for Innovation and Change Methodologies (IICM) change-key to structure the efforts of changing an organization. We then discuss a case study, highlighting how the interplay of the *what* and *how* support an organization in reaching its goals.

5.1 Participation and Engagement

Participation and engagement are invaluable in developing robustness in an organization. We find the discussions on open strategy helpful in framing our approach.

In the past, strategy processes were an activity for senior managers and their advisers, their internal or external strategy consultants, and were highly confidential. Open strategy consists of approaches among large groups within an organization as well as external stakeholders (Seidl, von Krogh, and Whittington 2019). Julian Birkinshaw (2017) from the London Business School argues that strategy-making has become considerably more open in recent years. *Openness* means who is involved and the transparency of how much information is shared. The benefits of open strategy are greater creativity, increased commitment, joint sensemaking, and favorable impression management (Hautz, Seidl, and Whittington 2017).

 | https://doi.org/10.1515/9783112242803-005

Information technology (IT) has also contributed to open strategy by allowing for digital and online formats that can include more participants than are usually possible in in-person workshops. Further, approaches to foresight such as scenario planning and business war-gaming, at least with respect to their workshop character, appear to be useful in the open strategy (Marsick and Watkins 2015).

In both scenario planning and business war-gaming, interactive workshops are conducive to explorations of the future. In scenario planning, the focus is on scanning a business or an industry's external environment and exploring alternative plausible pictures of the future. In contrast, business war-gaming focuses on understanding how the competitive landscape of an industry will change in the future. Kees van der Heijden (1996), an influential former head of scenario planning team at Royal Dutch/Shell, has called scenario planning the "art of strategic conversations." One can argue that at the core of both approaches, participants collectively make sense of their business environment by including perspectives of those involved. Open strategy can also be used to conduct research.

The robust leadership framework relies on inclusiveness and collaboration, which means that leaders need to include a broader range of members in the discussions that define the organization's values and how they should be enacted. For example, an organization should invite employees from different levels of the organization to discuss the role of trust in performing tasks and pursuing goals.

Our framework emphasizes that fostering organizational robustness requires following particular approaches and practices. These approaches and practices rely on a leader's ability to provide clarity and orientation to the organization and promote a shared understanding of its goals and values among its members. Openness and collaboration are thus central to our proposed framework for robust leadership.

Both openness and collaboration are fundamental to the open strategy approach. This approach stresses the many advantages of including broader groups in strategy-making, rather than leaving this task exclusively to leaders and top managers. Open strategy is inclusive and creative. In addition, it requires to consider *how* people are working together. And as we will discuss in our case study, the *how* and the *what* can support each other.

Of course, there are many more approaches or workshop settings that are well suited for fostering participation and engagement. Approaches like Design Thinking or Futures Literacy Labs, just to name a few, are of course also well suited in this respect. And of course this is also the purpose of our robust leadership framework, to provide a framework that can then be filled with other ideas and approaches.

However, we believe that in particular approaches that have a future focus are helpful. Often the future of an organization, but also among stakeholder groups, is perceived as an open space which allows for discussions beyond daily restrictions, like budgets or planning cycles, or organizational politics.

5.2 Embracing the Change-Key

For managing change, we work with our *change capabilities key* (Figure 21). This framework is based on the conviction that those affected by change must understand the change in accordance with its direction, the *what* and the *how*; they need the skills and competencies to find their way under changed conditions; they need leaders who act as role models, who set an example, by showing the desired new behavior; and they need structures and an organizational setup that rewards the changed behavior. In the following, we will investigate the change capabilities key.

Understanding and Motivation: Members of an organization who are affected by organizational change need to understand why things are changing. This helps to overcome denial or a sense of loss and puts the focus on the advantages of change. Those affected should be motivated to support the change, by giving them a clear vision of what good is supposed to come out of the change. Only with this shared understanding, an alignment of supporting behavior of those affected is possible.

Skills and Competencies: Based on understanding and motivation of the members of an organization, the right skills and competencies need to be fostered, so that the change can be implemented and the organization is enabled to operate and act successfully in the new, changed environment.

Leadership and Role Modeling: Leaders are crucial for successful organizational change. Both top and middle management needs to model the new, changed behavior they want to see in their employees, to give security and orientation, and to motivate employees to emulate it.

Structures and Organization: Finally, structures like target systems, organizational structures, and company agreements need to be implemented to maintain the changes. All these structures need to point in the new direction. For example, if a company wants to become an innovator in its industry, but its target system fails to reward or even mention behavior that drives innovation, employees will not be motivated to foster innovation; they might even be frustrated at the end of the target system cycle.

The change-key has several functions. The framework opens up a dialogue on what is needed for successful change. It suggests the need to consider all elements

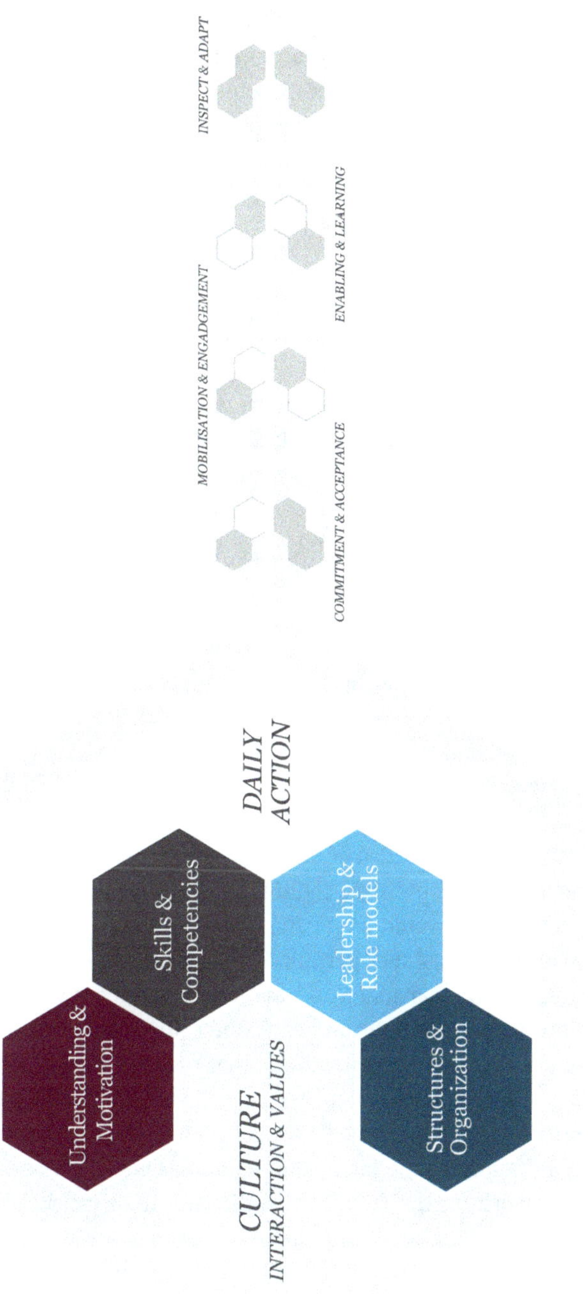

Figure 21: The IICM change-key.

for a holistic design of change processes and it is a practical tool in change management. It can be used to structure a change architecture; as a basis for interview questions for a preliminary assessment of the status quo at the beginning of a change process; or to measure the progress of organizational change.

5.3 Case Study

In this section, we describe a case that demonstrates how the *what* and *how* of the robust leadership framework supports an organization's change effort. We present a case study based on a consulting project at a financial services firm in which we were involved. The project lasted 18 months, from first contact with the client until project completion. To protect its confidentiality, we refer to the firm as Financia. It is a midsized regional bank in Germany with approximately 800 employees.

5.3.1 Starting Position

At the point of engagement, Financia had merged with another bank from its region 5 years prior. The discussion of scenario engagement started when a new CEO who had worked in the bank for most of his career was appointed. A new external board member was also appointed, and a third board member was close to retirement.

This engagement started with the idea of using scenarios to understand what the future of the financial services industry could look like in 10 years and what the implications of these changes would be for the bank and consequently for its strategy. In these early discussions, issues pertaining to culture were often raised. Specifically, these conversations pertained to how board members worked together and how they interacted with division heads, their direct subordinates. In addition, the perception of the board members was that regardless of which scenarios would develop or what the implications would be for the bank, the institution would need to undergo significant organizational change, which would itself require better collaboration among the leadership team. In light of these discussions, it was decided to work on the future of the financial services industry while addressing the culture of the bank. The decision was made to work on the values of the bank and on how these values can be practiced in daily work. In other words, both the *what* and the *how* of the robust leadership framework were addressed in this project at the same time.

5.3.2 Project Description

The project started out with two main workstreams: (1) strategy and scenarios (*what*); and (2) culture and change (*how*) (Figure 22).

Both workstreams were conducted in parallel with the same group of managers. This group consisted of 3 board members, 12 division heads, and 10 employees from different divisions of the bank. Some of them had leadership responsibility. These two workstreams were accompanied by internal communication measures.

Before the workstreams started, all board members and their direct subordinates were interviewed. The interviews had a twofold purpose: (1) to assess what the interviewees perceived as challenges for the industry; and (2) to identify what interviewees perceived as the relevant values of the organization as a proxy for understanding the organizational culture and assessing the style of collaboration within the organization.

Phase 1: Setting the Scene

One purpose of this phase was to enable the managers to start working together productively. Another purpose was to have initial discussions concerning the future of the financial services industry and the company's culture and values. The strategy and scenarios workstream developed scenarios to use as frameworks to think about innovations and new business models, assisting the bank in achieving a favorable long-term position. This part of the project adopted the scenario-building approach of the intuitive logics school, influenced by Royal Dutch Shell (Wilkinson and Kupers 2014).

Interviews with external stakeholders had two parts: understanding what interviewees considered the trends shaping the future of the financial services industry; and asking interviewees to describe the values of the organization. Furthermore, external data on trends concerning the future of the financial services industry were collected. From the interviews and external research, trends were synthesized, and a collection of organizational values was derived. This material served as the starting point for the first workshop.

This first workshop addressed elements taken from the strategy and scenarios and the culture and change workstreams. Participants reflected on the collection of values and focused on trends, for which the task was to assess (a) the relevance of trends concerning the future of the financial services industry and (b) the uncertainty involved in those trends. (If there were several possible directions, a high degree of uncertainty was indicated.) In the culture and change workstream, the aim for the project was to arrive at an agreement on company

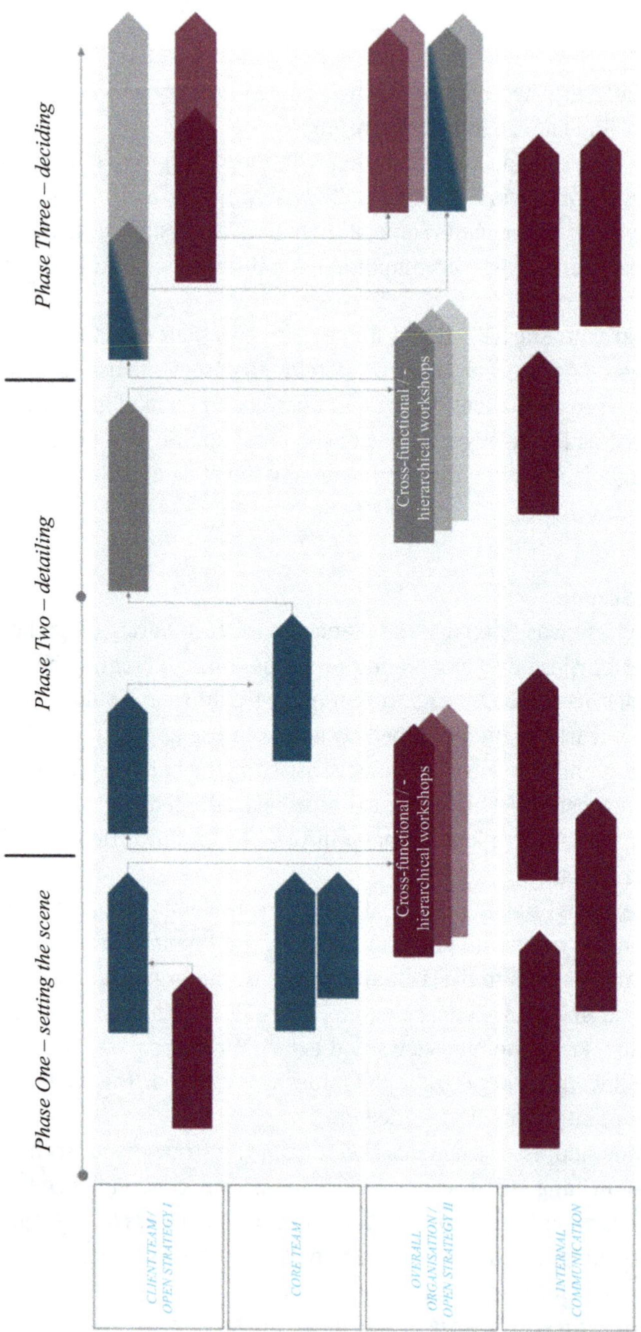

Figure 22: Workstreams of the project.
Blue: strategy and scenarios (what), Red: culture and change (how), Grey: business-modell & innovation.

values and to agree on how those values should be practiced within the organization and what mechanisms should be in place to ensure constant reflection concerning the implementation of these values in the organization.

Two daylong workshops were conducted during this phase. In the first workshop, the setting was noticeably unfamiliar to the participants. They were uncomfortable speaking openly about strategic matters, not only with fellow board members and division heads but also with employees. The CEO, however, emphasized the importance of including additional members of the organization in the process and asked everyone for open and candid discussion. Over the duration of the project, it was observable that this group, which remained the same throughout the project, worked progressively better together and had increasingly open conversations.

By the end of this phase, 5 workshops with 20 participants each had been held. The aim of these workshops was to share the outcomes of the first trends workshop and the first draft of company values with members of the organization. Each workshop was opened by a board member and accompanied by two division heads to show appreciation for employee involvement and to engage in the discussion and to start collecting feedback.

Phase 2: Detailing

The second phase of the project reflected on cross-functional and cross-hierarchical workshops and continued to detail scenarios and engage in discussions concerning innovations and new business models arising the context of the scenarios. This goal was achieved in the course of three workshops: Generating scenarios (1 day); detailing scenarios (1 day); and working on innovations and new business models (2 days). During this phase, no further workshops on culture and change were conducted. By the end of this phase, 5 open workshops, each with 20 participants had been conducted. The setup for these cross-functional and cross-hierarchical workshops was the same as that described for Phase 1, focusing on sharing scenarios and collecting ideas concerning innovations and new business models.

Phase 3: Deciding

While aggregation of the input from the cross-functional and cross-hierarchical workshops was performed at the beginning of this phase, the main aim of this phase was to make decisions in two ways: (1) to clarify the strategy going forward and allocate resources to new fields and (2) to agree on set of corporate values and clarify how the organization should practice those values.

Two workshops were conducted: one to decide on vision and new business models (1.5 days) and the other to clarify what changes should be made and sustained (1 day) based on the value discussions.

While the project was accompanied by ongoing internal communication with regard to both values and scenarios, subsequent workshops were conducted by team leaders to ensure the relevance of the values for each team within the organization.

5.3.3 Effects of Working on the What and the How in Parallel

The aim of discussing external forces and trends in scenario planning is to involve managers in creating a shared understanding of the challenges in their industry, including challenging their own assumptions about its future. This involvement is what happened in the first phase of the project, embracing participation and engagement.

At this point, participating managers had already discussed what the values of the company were or should be and how they should be practiced. When it came to discussing relevant trends for the future of their industry, these discussions were already more open because the group not only started to discuss what they would like to achieve in the future but also how they would like to achieve these goals in terms of how they would want to work together.

At the end of this first workshop, the entire group came together and started reflecting on the discussions and the process thus far. In regard to the blockchain trend, for example, some participants admitted they did not know enough about this technology to build scenarios. It appeared that this open admission of a lack of knowledge had been enabled by the group through previous discussions of the need for trusting, open, and respectful conversation.

The last workshop of this project was expected to lead to friction and arguments. This workshop concerned the allocation of resources to new projects, which naturally also meant diverting these resources away from existing workstreams. From the beginning of the project, the leadership team feared that this workshop would trigger old patterns of less trust and collaboration, which would hinder the development and implementation of a new strategy.

However, this workshop proceeded without undue tension. Two factors contributed to this outcome. All participants had a shared understanding not only of the future of their industry but also of the challenges for their own bank. In addition, by working on corporate values and how they should be practiced, participants found common ground for working together and making difficult decisions.

The entire project and especially the last workshop demonstrated to us that the *what* and the *how* can support each other in reaching a goal. While our empirical investigation of robust leadership showed that high trust has a positive impact on strategy, this case demonstrates the power of bringing together these two elements of our robust leadership framework.

Key takeaways from this chapter:

- To become a robust organization, participation and engagement of a broad range, or as much as possible, of members of an organization is paramount.
- Organizational levels cannot be separated from each other; ideally they should support each other.
- Similarly, the *what* and the *how* are interviewed.
- The IICM change-key is a means of structuring the change efforts in an organization.
- The case study demonstrates that combining the *what* and *how* in an organization sets the stage for successful transformation.

---

6 Assessing the Robustness of Leaders and Organizations

Questions addressed in this chapter:
- What have we found in our empirical investigation of robustness?
- How robust is your organization?
- How robust are you as a leader?
- How robust is your leadership style?

In this chapter, we explain what we have found in our empirical investigations on robust leadership. We then present our assessment tool so that you can quickly assess the robustness of your organization and of your personal style of leadership.

Based on our empirical investigation (Figure 23), 7% of the respondents described the leadership in their company as "robust." Although 6% described their leadership as "fragile," we were surprised to see that the majority assessed leadership as neither good nor bad. We labeled this category of respondents as "stuck in the middle." Considering that businesses operate in a dynamic environment, any organization whose leadership is "fragile" will need to strengthen it. However, organizations that are "stuck in the middle" are in a danger zone. With a leader who only partially meets some of the organization's demands, the organization may be falsely reassured that the leader is tending satisfactorily to emerging issues and

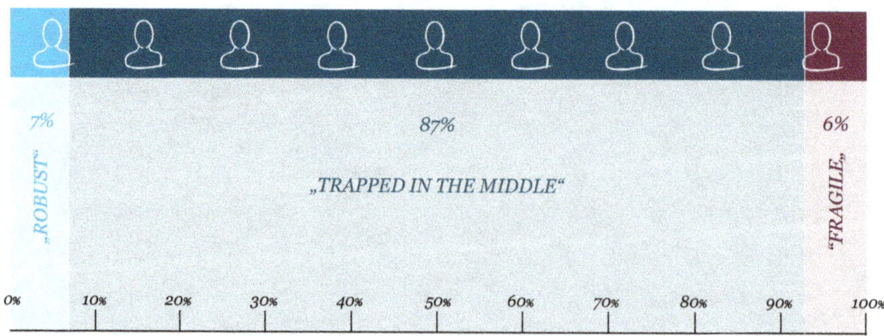

Figure 23: Robust leadership assessment.
Note: A weighted average of the elements of the robust leadership framework was calculated.

 | https://doi.org/10.1515/9783112242803-006

problems. If the organization's environment becomes more dynamic, or even volatile, false reassurance could prove problematic.

Key takeaways from this chapter:

- Only few participants in our robust leadership survey describe the leadership culture in their organization as robust.
- Nearly equal number of respondents report on "fragile" leadership culture.
- However, the vast majority described their leadership culture as "stuck in the middle," with signs of robustness but much room for improvement.

Our robust leadership assessment tool is below. The tool will allow you to assess and reflect on the robustness of your organization.

Again, you can do this assessment by yourself, or with your team or colleagues. Maybe you want to fill out the assessment individually and share the results in your team or with colleagues in a group discussion.

Robust Leadership Assessment Tool

***What?* Strategy and foresight**	**Questions should be answered on a scale of 1–5 (strongly disagree, disagree, neutral, agree, strongly agree)**
Imagining	We systematically utilize a range of formal methods (such as scenario analysis and roadmapping) to create alternative future outlooks.
	The organization is open, bringing external information into the company and maintaining an external network are encouraged.
	We are not afraid to reflect critically on the shared assumptions we have about our market, customers, and the way we do business.
	Leaders in our organization provide space for creative thinking.
Sensing	Our sensors ensure that we detect 80% of all trends that will shape our industry in the next 5–10 years.
	Our leaders are able to sense business opportunities and risks before they fully materialize to challenge the status quo.
	Leaders have been trained to sense new business opportunities and how to challenge established business models in the industry and in our firm.

(continued)

What? **Strategy and foresight**	**Questions should be answered on a scale of 1–5 (strongly disagree, disagree, neutral, agree, strongly agree)**
Transferring	In my organization we translate creative thinking (e.g., design thinking) into actual products or services.
	In my organization we translate strategy into definite projects.
	Leaders in our organization are able to adapt to changes in the business environment and to reconfigure resources accordingly.
	Faced with uncertainties in our business environment, leaders in our organization do not hesitate to take strategic decisions.
	Leaders in our organization formulate a clear vision and are able to translate the vision into tangible strategic goals for the individual.
	Leaders have been trained in making decisions under uncertainty and also perceive uncertainty in our industry as a source of opportunities.
	Leaders have been trained in adapting to changes in the environment and reconfiguring resources accordingly.
How? **Values and culture**	
Trust	Employees in our organization experience that leaders actively show their appreciation for the work being done and for other initiatives being proposed.
	Leaders in our organization create an atmosphere in which failure is perceived as a valuable opportunity to learn.
	Leaders in our organization succeed to create a strong identity that we are “in this together” and stay protectively in front of their team.
	Leaders in our organization foster the sense of individual meaning and contribution to common goals.
Openness	Employees in our organization are encouraged by their leaders to communicate cross-functionally and cross-hierarchically.
	Leaders in our organization stimulate open and transparent communication by introducing supportive communication structures.
	Leaders in our organization encourage critical thinking and raising challenging issues.
	Employees in our organization profit from an atmosphere created by their leaders that promotes an open exchange of ideas, feelings, and concerns.

(continued)

What? **Strategy and foresight**	**Questions should be answered on a scale of 1–5 (strongly disagree, disagree, neutral, agree, strongly agree)**
Development	Leaders in our organization invite open and constructive feedback.
	Leaders in our organization regularly provide context and orientation for decisions, goals, tasks, and responsibilities.
	Leaders in our organization support the long-term development of employees by providing time and guidance.
	Leaders in our organization utilize and foster the unique skills and talents of their employees in respect to the overall goal of the company.
	Leaders in our organization encourage employees to be attentive to trends and new developments in the industry.
Accountability	In our organization, we are aware that leaders and employees have specific roles and responsibilities and we live up to them.
	Leaders in our organization ensure employee accountability by continuously re-instantiating a shared understanding of the goals and tasks (e.g., through briefing and backbriefing).
	Leaders and employees in our organization meet as equals and have mutual trust that the other is meeting their responsibilities.
Final reflection	
	Leaders in our organization understand the relevance of values for foresight (perceiving changes).
	Leaders in our organization understand the relevance of values for the strategy of the organization.

If you want to benchmark your assessment or get our feedback, please consult our online assessment:

www.robust-leadership.com

7 Conclusion: Becoming a Robust Leader

Questions addressed in this chapter:
- How can tensions in leadership be addressed?
- How can I become a robust leader?
- What's next?

In this book, we have discussed the tensions that arise for leaders in a VUCA environment. We have described our robust leadership framework and its elements. And we have outlined, while reflecting our empirical investigations, what it takes to become not only a robust leader but also a robust organization.

In this concluding chapter, we want to do two things. We want to discuss how our robust leadership framework addresses the described tensions. Then we will share some thoughts on other ways our framework can be used.

7.1 Addressing Leadership Tensions

How does our robust leadership framework address leadership tensions? While doing the reflection exercises, you have probably asked yourself about this question. However, as we are not claiming that these are the only tensions that will arise, this discussion will also highlight, how our framework can be used. Again, keep in mind that the beauty of a framework is that it can be adapted and developed.

We identified four tensions in our robust leadership studies, two each addressing the organizational and individual or leadership level, as depicted in Figure 24.

We will start our discussion on the organizational level. The *linear and stable versus agile* tension is best addressed in the *what* part of the framework. In fast-changing business environments with a high degree of uncertainty concerning the future, organizations need to remain agile to cope with changes and even disruptions. However, it is also necessary to provide orientation. What is the organization's long-term vision and strategy? These questions can be answered through applying foresight. And while admittedly much is changing and global crises seem to be breaking out faster than ever, we must also admit that many developments like digitalization and sustainability have been around for decades. That we now see companies filing for bankruptcy and blaming digital disruptions actually means that management has been ignoring important developments in their

 | https://doi.org/10.1515/9783112242803-007

ORGANIZATIONAL

LINEAR & STABLE VS. AGILE

CULTURE VS. STRATEGY

LEADERSHIP

TRUST VS. GUIDELINES

AUTHENTICITY VS. CONFORMITY

Figure 24: Four leadership tensions.

market for a long time. Applying strategy and strategic foresight supports organizations in developing sensors to detect changes in their business environment early but also to use formats, such as scenario planning or business war-gaming, to challenge the assumptions in an organization.

Our robust leadership framework addresses the *culture versus strategy* tension. Our empirical investigation has demonstrated that a culture characterized by a high degree of trust leads to better strategies or strategic discussions. In addition, the case that we described in this book underlines the relevance of balancing culture and strategy.

Richard Whittington from the Said Business School at the University of Oxford has argued that when executives work together on strategy, a key pitfall is that they act hastily instead of clearly defining the challenges ahead (Schwarz

2020). He refers to the crux to describe a three-part strategic skill: (1) judging which issues are important and which ones are secondary; (2) judging how difficult it is to deal with these issues; and (3) focusing on these issues to avoid spreading resources too thin.

And, of course, a prerequisite is to have clear understanding of what strategy and foresight and values and culture are. Leaders need to make explicit what these concepts mean and of course also how they should be lived and executed. If a strategy is not long-term oriented and not sufficient foresight has been developed, not sufficient orientation is provided for the members of an organization and therefore the *what* and the *how* of our robust leadership framework are not in balance. Although it is a challenge, this calls for ambidextrous organization capable of doing several things at the same time: strategy and culture and bringing them into balance.

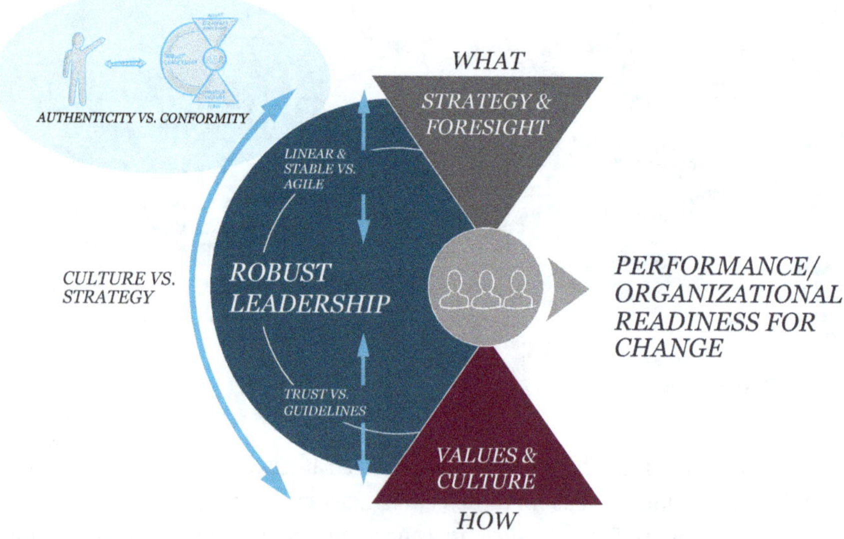

Figure 25: Robust leadership framework: addressing tensions.

Let us now turn to the individual level: that of the leader. We identified *trust versus guidelines* as leadership tension and we have discussed not only the importance of values and culture but above all the role of trust. However, in the corporate context, we see an increase in guidelines, whether on the top level in regard to corporate governance guidelines or in terms of who has authority to sign a purchasing order. Striking a balance is crucial. How much trust can I, as a leader, provide while ensuring respect for organizational guidelines? From our point of view, moving through our value pyramid is essential. Just providing trust as a leader is not sufficient. Openness and transparency are crucial to allow an employee to understand what the purpose of trust is and linking it to transparency.

For a leader, *authenticity versus conformity* can be even more daunting. If I as a leader can be characterized as “control-freak,” instilling trust is difficult. We experienced this when helping organizations to establish new ways of working in the post COVID-19 environment. Leaders who are comfortable walking around the office and looking over the shoulders of their team members to see what they are working on struggle with remote work.

So how can they actually instill trust and conform to the ways of working at their organization, while staying authentic? For us, making this tension explicit is a first step, discussing this tension with peers or a leader; at the end of the day, we all have someone above us. And moving on in our value pyramid, this is an issue of openness and transparency.

7.2 Working with the Framework

If we look back on the history of big corporate failures, the missing balance between the *what* and *how*, as framed in our robust leadership framework, becomes evident. The downfall of the iconic brand Kodak is often associated with the company’s failure to acknowledge the rise of digital photography, when the opposite is true. Kodak was one of the first firms to file patents for digital photography, exercising remarkable foresight. However, Kodak was unable to evolve from a high-margin film-producing company to a low-margin digital equipment company (Krupp and Schoemaker 2014). A similar perspective can be taken on the decline of the Encyclopedia Britannica. What this implies is that strategy and foresight, the *what*, is not enough to have an impact. The *what* needs to be in balance with the *how*, how members of an organization want to work together to transform their organization.

Others have previously argued for the necessity for strategic thinking in leadership, emphasizing the relevance of developing foresight (Greenstein 2017). While we absolutely agree with this perspective, our robust leadership framework does even more. Confronted with VUCA environments, any change in a strategy or the objective to become more innovative implies that an organization needs to change. And this implies that leaders need to think about how they want to change an organization and how they want to enable change. For us, values play a central role. Leaders need to deliberately use values to enable empowerment and collaboration in many ways.

We hope that this book is a starting point in fostering robust leadership. Our experiences with robust leadership workshops underline that the in this book included reflection exercises are a good starting point when used in groups.

But this is not enough. We were not surprised to see that our studies of robust leadership have revealed that training in some of the key areas of the robust leadership framework is underdeveloped. Usually, leaders have climbed the ladder because of a functional expertise they possess, such as being good in product development, accounting, or marketing. However, being a leader means leading an organization and for this very different skills are required. One observation we have made in our many years of consulting and training is that the more members of an organization are hierarchically speaking away from strategic decisions, the more they think that complex questions have easy answers. The closer they get, the more they are challenged with the complexity of an organization.

In other words, training and development are crucial for fostering individual and organizational robustness. Empirical evidence suggests that if leaders have been trained in decision-making under uncertainty or in developing foresight, the respective organization is more likely to exercise dynamic capabilities (Schwarz, Rohrbeck, and Wach 2020), which is crucial for an organization to stay in tune with the changes in their business environment.

Gary Hamel and Michele Zanini (2020) have argued that truly resilient organizations do the following:

- Never take refuge in denial
- Rush to meet the future
- Change before it had to
- Continually redefine customer expectations
- Capture more than its fair share of new opportunities
- Never experience an unanticipated earning shock
- Grow faster than its rivals
- Attract the world's most dynamic employees

While we would rather refer to robustness than resilience, our robust leadership framework supports organization in achieving these aims, and supports individual leaders in understanding how they can contribute to the robustness of an organization by becoming robust themselves.

The final reflection questions in our study on Robust Leadership were as follows:

1. Leaders in our organization understand the relevance of values for foresight (perceiving changes).
2. Leaders in our organization understand the relevance of values for the strategy of the organization.

For both, we saw a positive notion in the survey of around 60%. This is a good sign that balancing strategy and foresight and values and culture in organizations is understood, at least among the larger organizations that we surveyed. However, understanding is just one side of the coin. Developing and living the necessary skills, and becoming robust on an organizational and individual level is the other. And this is where our robust leadership assessment has room for improvement.

Our robust leadership framework is a work in progress. We'd love to hear from you! How have you used the framework? What were your experiences? What is your take on the robust leadership assessment tool? Please reach out, so that we can keep developing robust leadership!

References

Birkinshaw, Julian and Cristina Gibson. 2004. “Building Ambidexterity into an Organization.” *MIT Sloan Management Review* 45(June).

Birkinshaw, Julian. 2017. Reflections on open strategy. *Long Range Planning, 50*(3), 423–426. https://doi.org/https://doi.org/10.1016/j.lrp.2016.11.004.

Brown, Brené. 2018. *Dare to Lead: Brave Work. Tough Conversations. Whole Hearts.* New York: Random House.

Brown, Tim. 2009. *Change by Design: How Design Thinking Transforms Organizations and Inspires Innovation.* New York: Harper-Collins.

Bungay, Stephen. 2011. *Art of Action: How Leaders Close the Gaps Between Plans, Actions and Results.* Boston: Nicholas Brealey Publishing.

Chamorro-Premuzic, Tomas. 2020. “How to Spot an Incompetent Leader.” Harvard Business Review. https://hbr.org/2020/03/how-to-spot-an-incompetent-leader?utm_m. . .eeklyhotlist_not_activesubs&referral=00202&deliveryName=DM72830.

Day, George S. and Paul J. H. Schoemaker. 2019. *See Sooner, Act Faster: How Vigilant Leaders Thrive in an Era of Digital Turbulence.* Management on the Cutting Edge. Cambridge: MIT Press.

Day, George S. and Paul J. H. Schoemaker. 2006. *Peripheral Vision: Detecting the Weak Signals That Will Make or Break Your Company*. Boston: Harvard Business School Press.

Denning, Steve. 2018. *The Age of Agile: How Smart Companies Are Transforming the Way Work Gets Done.* New York: AMACOM.

Dirks, Kurt and Donald Ferrin. 2002. “Trust in Leadership: Meta-Analytic Findings and Implications for Research and Practice.” *The Journal of Applied Psychology* 87 (September): 611–628. https://doi.org/10.1037//0021-9010.87.4.611.

Doerr, John. 2018. *Measure What Matters: How Google, Bono, and the Gates Foundation Rock the World with OKRs*. Penguin Publishing Group.

Drucker, Peter F. 1969. *The Age of Discontinuity: Guidelines to Our Changing Society*. London: Heinemann.

Frei, Frances and Anne Morriss. 2020. “Begin with Trust: The First Step to Becoming a Genuinely Empowering Leader.” *Harvard Business Review*. https://hbr.org/2020/05/begin-with-trust.

Gerstner, Louis V. 2003. *Who Says Elephants Can’t Dance?: Leading a Great Enterprise Through Dramatic Change*. New York: HarperCollins.

Gharajedaghi, Jamshid. 1999. *Systems Thinking*. Boston: Butterworth Heinemann.

Gordon, Adam Vigdor, Lasse Jonasson and Nicklas Larsen. 2021. “Organizational Future-Preparedness After Covid-19: A Clearer Role for the Board?” Copenhagen Institute for Futures Studies

Gotsis, George and Katerina Grimani. 2016. “The Role of Servant Leadership in Fostering Inclusive Organizations.” *Journal of Management Development* Gotsis, George: ggotsis@phs.uoa.gr: Emerald Group Publishing Limited. https://doi.org/10.1108/JMD-07-2015-0095.

Greenstein, Shane. 2017. “The Reference Wars: Encyclopædia Britannica’s Decline and Encarta’s Emergence.” *Strategic Management Journal* 38 (5): 995–1017. https://doi.org/10.1002/smj.2552.

Hamel, Gary and Michele Zanini. 2020. *Humanocracy: Creating Organizations as Amazing as the People Inside Them*. Boston: Harvard Business Review Press.

Hamel, Gary and C. K. Prahalad. 1994. *Competing for the Future*. Boston: Harvard Business School Press.

Heijden, Kees Van der. 2005. *Scenarios: The Art of Strategic Conversation*. Chichester: Wiley.

 | https://doi.org/10.1515/9783112242803-008

Johnson, Gerry, Kevan Scholes and Richard Whittington. 2006. *Exploring Corporate Strategy*. Harlow: FT Prentice Hall.

Jong, Rob-Jan de. 2015. *Anticipate: The Art of Leading by Looking Ahead*. New York: AMACOM.

Jordan, Jennifer, Michael Wade and Elizabeth Teracino. 2020. "Every Leader Needs to Navigate These 7 Tensions." *Harvard Business Review*. https://hbr.org/2020/02/every-leader-needs-to-navigate-these-7-tensions.

Kotter, John P. 2012. *Leading Change*. Harvard Business Publishing. Boston: Harvard Business Review Press.

Krupp, Steven and Paul J. H. Schoemaker. 2014. *Winning the Long Game: How Strategic Leaders Shape the Future*. New York: Public Affairs.

Krupp, Steve. 2020. "From Blame to Gain: Leading with Agility in a Crisis." Heidrick & Struggles. 2020. https://www.heidrick.com/Knowledge-Center/Publication/from_blame_to_gain_leading_with_agility_in_a_crisis.

Latham, Gary and Craig Pinder. 2005. "Work Motivation Theory and Research at the Dawn of the Twenty-First Century." *Annual Review of Psychology* 56 (February): 485–516. https://doi.org/10.1146/annurev.psych.55.090902.142105.

Leinwand, Paul and Cesare R. Mainardi. 2016. *Strategy That Works: How Winning Companies Close the Strategy-to-Execution Gap*. Boston: Harvard Business Review Press.

Lencioni, Patrick M. 2010. *The Five Dysfunctions of a Team: A Leadership Fable*. San Francisco: Wiley.

Markides, Constantinos C. 2021. *Organizing for the New Normal: Prepare Your Company for the Journey of Continuous Disruption*. London: Kogan Page.

Marsick, Victoria J. and Karen E. Watkins. 2015. *Informal and Incidental Learning in the Workplace*. London: Routledge.

Mayer, Roger C., James H. Davis and F. David Schoorman. 1995. "An Integrative Model of Organizational Trust." *The Academy of Management Review* 20 (3): 709–734. https://doi.org/10.2307/258792.

Pfeffer, Jeffrey. 2015. *Leadership BS: Fixing Workplaces and Careers One Truth at a Time*. New York: Harper Collins.

Ramirez, Rafael and Angela Wilkinson. 2016. *Strategic Reframing: The Oxford Scenario Planning Approach*. Oxford: Oxford Publishing.

Renjen, Punit Renjen. 2020. "The Heart of Resilient Leadership: Responding to COVID-19." Deloitte, https://www.deloitte.com/us/en/insights/topics/economy/covid-19/heart-of-resilient-leadership-responding-to-covid-19.html.

Rohrbeck, René, Cinzia Battistella and Eelko Huizingh. 2015. "Corporate Foresight: An Emerging Field with a Rich Tradition." *Technological Forecasting and Social Change* 101 (December): 1–9. https://doi.org/10.1016/j.techfore.2015.11.002.

Rumelt, Richard P. 2022. *The Crux: How Leaders Become Strategists*. London: Profile.

Schawbel, Dan. 2015. "Jeffrey Pfeffer: What Most People Don't Know About Leadership." *Forbes* 2015.

Schon, Donald A. 2008. *The Reflective Practitioner: How Professionals Think In Action*. Basic Books.

Schoemaker, Paul J. H. and Robert E. Gunther. 2002. *Profiting from Uncertainty: Strategies for Succeeding No Matter What the Future Brings*. New York: Free Press.

Schoemaker, Paul J. H. 2020. "Are You Ready for the Next Big Shock?" Inc. 2020.

Schwarz, Jan Oliver and Rupert Hofmann. 2019. "Is Today's Science Fiction Tomorrow's Science Fact? On the Relevance of Science-Fiction for Trend Research: Insights from the Audi Brand Fiction Space Project." The Foresight Academy, https://www.motivesandfiction.com/cms-media/media-3952720.pdf.

Schwarz, Jan Oliver. 2020. "Revisiting Scenario Planning and Business Wargaming from an Open Strategy Perspective." *World Futures Review* 12 (3): 291–303. https://doi.org/10.1177/1946756720953182.

– – – . 2023. *Strategic Foresight: An Introductory Guide to Practice*. London" Taylor & Francis.

Schwarz, Jan Oliver, René Rohrbeck and Bernhard Wach. 2020. "Corporate Foresight as a Microfoundation of Dynamic Capabilities." *FUTURES & FORESIGHT SCIENCE* 2 (2): e28. https://doi.org/https://doi.org/10.1002/ffo2.28.

Scoblic, J. Peter. 2020. Learning from the Future. Harvard Business Review. https://hbr.org/webinar/2020/12/learning-from-the-future.

Scott, Kim. 2019. *Radical Candor: Fully Revised & Updated Edition: Be a Kick-Ass Boss without Losing Your Humanity*. New York: St. Martin's Publishing Group.

Seidl, David, Georg von Krogh und Richard Whittington. 2019. *Cambridge Handbook of Open Strategy*. Cambridge: Cambridge University Press.

Sinek, Simon. 2011. *Start with Why: How Great Leaders Inspire Everyone to Take Action*. London: Penguin Books Limited.

Stamoulis, Dean and Erika Mannion. 2012. "Making It to the Top: Nine Attributes That Differentiate CEOs." Russell Reynolds Associates. 2012. https://www.russellreynolds.com/insights/thought-leadership/making-it-to-the-top-nine-attributes-that-differentiate-ceos.

Stillmann, Jessica. 2017. "How Reading Fiction Can Make You a Better Leader." Inc. 2017. https://www.inc.com/jessica-stillman/how-reading-fiction-can-make-you-a-better-leader.html.

Taleb, Nassim N. 2012. *Antifragile: How to Live in a World We Don't Understand*. New York: Random House.

van der Heijden, Kees. 1996. *Scenarios: The Art of Strategic Conversation*. Chichester: John Wiley & Sons.

Wilkinson, Andrea and Roland Kupers. 2013. Living in the Futures. *Harvard Business Review*, (5), 119–127.

World Economic Forum. 2020. "The Future of Jobs Report 2020." https://www.weforum.org/publications/the-future-of-jobs-report-2020/.

Yukl, Gary and William L. Gardner III. 2020. *Leadership in Organizations*. London: Pearson Education.

List of Figures

 | https://doi.org/10.1515/9783112242803-009

www.ingramcontent.com/pod-product-compliance
Lightning Source LLC
LaVergne TN
LVHW010616110826
845149LV00003B/935